Lake Christina

Cookbook

CHRISTINA INA ANKA
LAKE ASSOCIATION

Lake Christina Cookbook

Lake Christina Cookbook

The primary purpose of this cookbook is to share a whole host of wonderful game, fowl, and fish recipes provided by the members, family and friends of the Christina Ina Anka Lake Association. (Three lakes inter-connected: Christina, Ina and Anka)

West central Minnesota has a long tradition with outdoorsmen, fisherman, hunters and especially duck hunters, as this is part of the great "prairie pot hole region" where ducks and waterfowl are raised in the numerous sloughs, swamps, lakes and rivers.

What is the Christina, Ina, Anka lakeshore association? From here on, we will refer to our organization as the CIALA. Or simply CIA.

In 1999 a group of conservation minded duck hunters who were dismayed at the declining duck counts and overall decline of water quality of Lake Christina and surrounding duck-type lakes, decided to take action. They were determined to see if there would be any support for establishing a lake association with the intent of trying to reverse the trend of fewer and fewer ducks and the decline of habitat and water quality. They went around to the various cabins and old hunting shacks asking many of the locals who hunted this 4,000 acre shallow lake for their support. That first group of enthusiasts was headed up by Harvey Nelson (USFWS retired), Howard Norby, John Lindquist, Jim Knudsen, and Duke Anderson, with the support and enthusiasm of many others. The opening remarks from Tony Soderman allude to that very deep inner care and emotion many residents here have for the canvasback duck!

The Introduction and first few chapters are dedicated to the history of the lake and activities of the CIA. As you read it, you will undoubtedly become excited about the great results obtained by a dedicated bunch of folks whose heart and soul was just trying to make a difference and bring this watershed back to its strong traditions of waterfowl hunting.

The secondary purpose of the cookbook is to bring to the attention of waterfowlers everywhere, especially diving duck hunters, that Christina exists and is one of the most important habitat and staging areas for the mighty canvasback and other diving and puddle ducks. In fact, when this shallow lake is healthy, it holds up to 20% of the North American continent's population of canvasbacks during the fall and spring migration.

Finally, this book is a fundraiser to assist the CIA in continuing the restoration and improvement of habitat, duck numbers and water quality. All the proceeds of this cookbook will go back into solving and maintaining these lakes by the CIA, non-profit association 503C Corporation Tax ID #41196771

This cookbook is an unorthodox way of telling a story, providing a look into the hunting traditions of the past and offering well over 150 outdoor cooking recipes that come from people who love the outdoors, who enjoy eating game and know how to cook it. Over a three year period we asked all attendees of the September CIA fundraiser to bring in their favorite recipes for a free chance at a donated gun. We received numerous recipes and others that were copied from many sources. Whenever possible or known, credit is given to the originator of the offering. We hope you enjoy!

Brad Gruss
Author & Lake Christina Resident

Dedicated to our family

This cookbook is dedicated to our parents, Fremont and Karen Gruss. My father gave me the love of the outdoors and the shooting sports. Don and Sue Lee, for giving Teri the love for cooking. And to our sons, Chef Charlie Gruss and Andy Gruss and our black lab "Buckwheat" the Son of "Bear."

Dedicated to the CIA

The CIA is a dedicated group, with common goals and a cause. To all who have worked so hard to get us here today and future volunteers who will be needed to keep Lake Christina a viable resource for hunting and outdoor enjoyment.

"A love for the outdoors and for home-cooking are among life's greatest enjoyments passed from parents to children."

Teri Lee Gruss

Acknowledgements

Special thanks to: Dennis Anderson for sharing his two books, *"Ashby MN: The town that aspired to be a metropolis 1879-1979"* and *"125 years of Memories 1879-2004"* Grant County Historical Society. Both books provided the majority of the history. Paul Englund, writer for Minnesota Waterfowler Magazine, (Winter issue 1995). To our good friend, John House, for the beautiful front and back covers, for the wonderful illustrations, paintings and especially for his strong enthusiasm and commitment to Lake Christina.

Thanks also to: Harvey Nelson USFWS retired; Jon Schneider, Ducks Unlimited; Duke Anderson; Ethel Palmquist; John Lindquist; Tom and Pam Warnke; Greg and Gwen (Gradin) Lillemon; Lee Peterson; Ed Hentges; Loreli Westby and her father Dick Fihn for history and photographs; Tony, Tom and Sue Soderman; Gwen and Jim Risbrudt; Mark Deutschman, Houston Engineering; Mark Reineke, JOR Engineering; Tom Carlson, MNDNR; Steve Wick, Kevin Fick and Mel Bois, for taking the time to be interviewed and sharing their fond memories.

Thanks to DU and Lyman Products for allowing us to reproduce recipes brought in from the CIA members, who felt that these recipes in their publications were our members' favorites too! A warm feeling in our hearts will always be there for Joe Knutson, as he was the one that made it possible for us to live in this old cabin on the shores of Lake Christina! Thanks to all who participated in sharing their recipes, photos, history and comments.

Thanks also to Susan Mertes, Susan's Studio, for a wonderful job of editing and layout and to Dan Breyak of Catalyst Graphics for the guidance, contacts and encouragement (two unbelievably talented "book" people!).

Finally, Thank You! for buying this cookbook. We sincerely hope that this book will inspire you and your family to enjoy the rich history and traditions of hunting and fishing, to always have respect for the game you take, to honor the land and habitat, and to really enjoy a good home-cooked wild game dish.

CONTENTS

1   **Introduction**
Why Lake Christina? What YOU did not know!
By A.R. "Tony" Soderman

7   **Chapter 1**
Reflections on 70 years of tracking events on Lake Christina
By Harvey Nelson

17   **Chapter 2** - Canvasback: The King of Ducks and the Ducks Unlimited/ Lake Christina Partnership
By Jon Schneider, MN Ducks Unlimited Biologist

25   **Chapter 3**
Historic Hunting Traditions and the remaining hunting clubs

69   **Chapter 4** - Hunting the Bulrushes on Lake Christina
By John House (Two page lake map spread)

85   **Chapter 5** - Duck & Goose Recipes

104   **Chapter 6** - Big Game Recipes

125   **Chapter 7** - Upland Bird Recipes

141   **Chapter 8** - Fish Recipes

158   **Chapter 9** - Smoking Game and Fish

166   **Chapter 10** - Sides Dishes, Sauces

185   **Chapter 11** - Nutritional Aspects of Wild Game
By Teri Lee Gruss, MS Nutrition

191   **Chapter 12** - Making a Difference
By Brad B. Gruss

Illustrations & Artwork *by John House, local favorite artist and winner of the MN Grand Slam (first to win all MN state wildlife stamps)*

Lake Christina Cookbook

Introduction
WHY LAKE CHRISTINA?
What YOU did not know!
By A.R. "Tony" Soderman

Those who will read these pages share a common interest in Lake Christina located in west central Minnesota approximately 160 miles northwest of Minneapolis-St. Paul, with water in Douglas, Grant and Ottertail counties. Interest is shared by local residents, recreational visitors, seasonal waterfowlers, game and water biologists, scientists and a host of others. Everybody has their own insight and "knows" why Lake Christina is so important to each of us. But sadly, our well-intentioned effort to record the "history" comes nearly a century too late.

Today we try to "save" Lake Christina, each of us for our own well-articulated reasons. However, few people truly appreciate the historical significance of this body of water. Everyone knows the importance of the Mississippi River and the related importance of Lake Itasca where the river originates. Everyone knows the importance of Lake Superior for its size and relationship to international shipping and Lake Mille Lacs for recreational fishing. But few people (even those ardent waterfowlers contributing to these pages) realize the historical importance of this comparatively small body of water to migratory bird hunting on the North American continent.

Aldo Leopold and others introducing H. Albert Hochbaum's famous treatise *The Canvasback on a Prairie Marsh* (published by The American Wildlife Institute in 1944) explained:

> [T]he Canvasback is used as a "base datum" and ...we offer no apology for thus elevating the lordly Canvasback to a classical role, for among duck-minded

people he has long been the "gold standard" against which all lesser fry are weighed and measured. (p. xii)

The history of Lake Christina is inexorably tied to the "King of Ducks" – The Canvasback. We all "knew that." And, it is nothing new. In 1949, Walter L. Bush in describing the prairie lakes of Minnesota reported:

> Along this rather broad front, there are many localities that have become famous over the years ... Lake Christina and Pelican Lake near Ashby are famous canvasback and bluebill lakes. (*Wildfowling in the Mississippi Flyway*, edited by Eugene V. Connett, published by D. Van Nostrand Company, Inc., 1949, p. 146)

But few people know why. The simple answer is that Lake Christina was the turning point for migrating canvasbacks from the days before the eyes of white men ever saw them. Mallards are in Europe; canvasbacks are not. They nest in Canada and gather at Lake Winnipegosis 200 miles north of Winnipeg. Migrating "with the calendar rather than in response to any particular weather conditions" canvasbacks leave that region between October 10 and 12 and continue staging in the Delta Marsh. (Hochbaum, p. 128) Jimmy Robinson who did the Sports Afield Duck Survey for 50 years would call our hunting camp on Lake Christina to verify the arrival of the Cans in mid-October.

Canvasbacks did not migrate elsewhere. Canvasbacks migrated from the Delta Marsh to Lake Christina and then turned east ultimately reaching their winter grounds on the East Coast from Chesapeake Bay to the Susquehanna Flats.

The history of the canvasback migration explains the importance of Lake Christina. The United States Department of Interior compiled a lengthy volume entitled *Waterfowl Tomorrow* which was published in 1964. Explaining the migration pattern of the canvasback, Arthur S. Hawkins wrote:

> Canvasbacks have been crowded by civilization into one last corner of the flyway, northwestern Minnesota ...Great flights have not been seen in the last few years which, as recently as the mid-fifties, left Delta Marsh, Manitoba, in mid-October. They regathered first on Lake Christina in Minnesota, next on Lake Poygan in Wisconsin, then St. Clair Flats in Michigan, and finally on to winter grounds in Chesapeake Bay. (p. 204)

That is why you can read about market hunters setting up camps on Lake Christina or trainloads of scatter gunners coming up from the Twin Cities or as far away as Chicago to shoot from the train windows along the notorious "Hump Back" (the high ground between Lake Christina and Pelican Lake). Some names are famous in Lake Christina lore like Sam Fertig or one of the earliest settlers, Hans Palmquist. In the days of the market gunners, redheads were $3.50 per dozen while canvasbacks were $4.00 per dozen! If the King of Ducks was your interest, Lake Christina was one of your limited choices of destination!

Sure, you might find canvasbacks anywhere. One retired Lake Christina waterfowler bemoaned the fact that Cans were closed on Lake Christina but you could shoot four of them a day in Arizona. The only problem was that there had not been a canvasback bagged in Arizona since 1948! Fall snowstorms might blow them off course, but their traditional turning point was Lake Christina, and if you wanted to see Cans, that is where they went – all of them!

The importance of Lake Christina was well-known in the 1950s and its decline stimulated the first chemical treatment in November 1965. But it was not until July 1983 that the lake was officially designated a "Wildlife Management Lake" by Joe Alexander, then-Commissioner of the Minnesota Department of Natural Resources.

> "The struggle to hold back civilization and restore Lake Christina continues to the present, but it is more than a large project for a small area. It is a small project for an entire Continent!"

In the first edition of *Waterfowl Tomorrow*, affixed to the cover is a foldout map of North America that was prepared by the Department of the Interior Fish and Wildlife Service Bureau of Sport Fisheries and Wildlife.

That map of the entire continent tells the tale. All the famous old waterfowl haunts are there: Merrymeeting Bay, Great South Bay, Barnegat Bay, Susquehanna Flats, Back Bay, Currituck, South Louisiana Marshes, Reelfoot, Horseshoe Lake, Cheyenne Bottoms, Bear River Marshes, Klamath-Tule, Winnipegosis, Hudson Bay, James Bay, Delta Marsh, Netley Marsh and maybe 50 more. These are the greatest names in the history of North American waterfowl.

And there, right in the middle of the map, dead center (if you fold it in quarters) in the heart of North American waterfowling is the only spot in Minnesota – our beloved Lake Christina!

So, the next time you gaze across The Lake, pause for a moment and reflect upon your good fortune. You are among the privileged few who know Lake Christina and its storied history! Other famous haunts offer rich traditions, good hunting and storied histories, too. The difference? Lake Christina's got the Cans! It is not just a "famous Lake" or "great hunting spot." It is one of the MOST IMPORTANT LAKES IN THE HISTORY OF WATERFOWLING!

INTRODUCTION

Tony Soderman, my friend, gave me the first opportunity to hunt Christina in the late 1980s. Left to right: Mark Gerling, Tony Soderman, Brad Gruss, after hunting the Soderman Pass on Lake Christina — 10-25-94

LAKE CHRISTINA COOKBOOK

CHAPTER 1

Reflections on 70 Years of Tracking Events at Lake Christina

By Harvey K. Nelson USFWS (retired)

As a young lad, I grew up in and around Evansville, Minnesota. My father was a farmer through the drought of the mid-1930s, and then moved to Evansville to work for the Great Northern Railroad the remainder of his life. He also was a duck hunter, so I had an early start. I shot my first mallard on the Mahla slough at age 9, and began hunting on and around Lake Christina (Christina) when I was about 12 years old.

I had the pleasure of hunting on Christina with Horace "Barney" Norby, father of Howard and Bob Norby. I sort of grew up with those "kids." Barney taught me the art of shooting diving ducks over decoys. I remember clearly the first "bull can" I shot as he was coming into the decoys. That started "can fever" that is still with me today. In addition to shooting canvasbacks, redheads, bluebills (scaup) and ringbills (ring-necked ducks) on the Norby pass. We also did a lot of pass shooting along the railroad grade at the west end of the lake and at the top of the Seven Sisters Hills to the east, especially during stormy weather. I remember when the dam between Christina and Pelican Lake was built by the WPA program during the late 1930s to help maintain water in the lake for ducks. I continued my relationship with the Norby families over the years and watched many changes at Christina the past 70 years. I still spend a few days there each October and manage to shoot a few ducks, but today the better hunting is out in the rushes over decoys. Now, reminiscing about the "good old days," the camaraderie and just watching the coots and ducks is more important to me.

When reflecting on those early years, my love for the lakes, marshes, ducks and other wildlife, and the recognition of the importance of water during the drought years, had a profound influence on my life. In fact, "Barney" Norby was instrumental in encouraging me to go back to the University of Minnesota when I returned from World War II, and major in fish and wildlife management. As a result I had an interesting, challenging and productive career of 42 years with the U. S. Fish and Wildlife Service (USFWS), that involved a lot of work with wetlands and waterfowl throughout North America.

Over the years I maintained a keen interest in Christina and followed the status of fall waterfowl use and periodic changes in water levels and vegetation. While in graduate school I was a member of a Minnesota Conservation Department Lake Survey Crew that did one of the early aquatic plant surveys on Christina in 1949. During my years with USFWS I always kept an eye on Christina. While Director of the Northern Prairie Wildlife Research Center at Jamestown, ND we were able to support hydrological and limnological research on factors influencing fall waterfowl use of Christina. The initial work was done by Drs. Jim Grier and Malcolm ("Mac") Butler at North Dakota State University (NDSU). A major concern was how to maintain the water quality necessary to enhance production of sago pondweed and other submerged aquatic plants that provide important waterfowl food resources. Meanwhile, Christina was officially designated as a game lake in 1983, because of importance as a major fall staging area for migrating diving ducks, especially canvasbacks. When I returned to Minnesota in 1980, I was able to become more directly involved with Christina again in cooperation with the Minnesota Department of Natural Resources (MNDNR) staff and other organizations like the Minnesota Waterfowl Association, Ducks Unlimited, and NDSU.

CHAPTER 1

During the next 10 years a substantial ecological data base was developed for Christina by Tom Carlson, MNDNR Biologist; Mac Butler, Mark Hanson, Nichole-Hansel Welch and other graduate students from NDSU. Minnesota DNR staff also prepared the initial Christina Lake Management Plan. Reactivation of the Lake Christina Working Group in 2000 provided better interagency coordination and public involvement in lake management issues. An issue of major concern was to develop a current hydrologic budget for Christina, which also influences Anka, Ina and Pelican lakes. The first phase of this project was done by the U.S. Geological Survey in 2003 through a cooperative interagency funding arrangement, that included other conservation organizations, contributions by land owners and hunting clubs and special fund raising efforts. The broader watershed evaluation was put on hold. This effort resulted in development of a closer working relationship with the Pelican Lake Association. Further details on the results from many of the above investigations can be found in numerous agency and organization reports and University theses.

In general terms, shallow lakes like Christina undergo cyclic changes from a clear water state to a turbid state; depending on water levels and other factors causing turbidity such as quality of water inflow, wave action and rough fish populations. Initial management consisted of removing stop logs in the outlet structure to lower the water level to the authorized elevation when possible and periodic reduction of fish populations, as was done by chemical treatment in 1965, 1987 and 2003. Manipulation of water levels is influenced to a large degree by the water level maintained in adjacent Pelican Lake and the elevation of the outlet structure there. As more was learned about the ecology and hydrology of Christina and management practices (biomanipulation) required to improve water quality and production of aquatic food resources required by ducks in this lake and the surrounding area, it became apparent that a more systematic, unified and continuing approach was required. There needed to be a procedure whereby the property owners on Christina, Anka and Ina, and the community in general, could have a stronger voice in future management and use of these lakes, and maintain liaison with the Pelican Lake Association.

The obvious solution was to establish a lake association similar to the Pelican Lake Association and hundreds of similar lake associations for recreational fishing lakes and game (shallow) lakes throughout the state. I made this recommendation to the group of property owners on the three lakes that had participated in previous discussions, and offered to help organize a lake association. We had some preliminary meetings in the Twin Cities to determine the basic organizational requirements and how to proceed. Those primarily involved were John Lindquist, Jim Knudsen. Al Hanser, Jim Dayton, Vern Ostrom, Bill Larson, Howard Norby, Tony Soderman, Earl Oxley, Dean Elmer, Oscar Norgren, Denny Kumlin, Todd Thulen, Duke Anderson and John House. Others who became involved soon thereafter were Brad Gruss, Weldon Jacobsen, Mark Gerling, Robert Norby, Gene Eidem, Kevin Fick, Ron Youngdahl, Leroy Evavold and Tom Warnke.

We held the first public meeting in Melby, Minnesota on February 26, 1999, to discuss the merits of forming a lake association. There was a consensus to proceed. It was suggested that the organization be called the Christina, Ina, Anka Lake Association or "CIA." The first membership meeting was held in Melby on April 29, 2001, at which the Mission Statement and Articles of Incorporation were adopted, and the initial working groups/committees were established. A Board of Directors was subsequently established and "CIALA" was up and running. The first Board members were John Lindquist,

CHAPTER 1

President; Jim Knudsen, Secretary/Treasurer; Dean Elmer, Tod Thulen, Howard Norby, Denny Kumlin and Jim Dayton. I continued to serve as an adviser. Board members have changed over the years as membership and interest increased. The present Board members are listed in the back of this book.

The challenge then was to:
(1) Further define the role and responsibilities of the CIALA.
(2) Identify priority issues related to these lakes and Pelican Lake.
(3) Develop a program structure through partnership arrangements to begin addressing these issues and corrective measures required to address these problems in a systematic manner.
(4) Develop an internal and external communications network to keep members and the public informed.
(5) Build a financial and political support base to accomplish these tasks.

Such actions are progressing well and accomplishments to date have been substantial. The details can be found in minutes of Board meetings, periodic CIA Newsletters and other reports on file.

Of the original committees established, the Fund Raising/Banquet Committee and the Water Management Committee have been the most active. Duke Anderson has led the water management group, and has been the local "Sparkplug" for exploring other alternatives to maintaining lower lake levels when necessary, including the recent investigation of pumping facilities by Houston Engineering.

In retrospect, establishment of the CIA Lake Association was a careful and wise decision made by the initial group of concerned property owners on the three lakes, with strong support from other interested parties. It has been successful because of the dedicated Board of Directors, the members and other volunteers who stepped up to the plate to help make things happen from day one. An important factor was the increased public understanding and support. This positive action provided a recognized organizational structure for concerned citizens to systematically address management problems in the three principal lakes that comprise the Lake Christina watershed, and relationships to adjacent Pelican Lake and its watershed. It also provided a better mechanism for working with state and federal agencies, other conservation organizations and local units of government. The primary goals and specific management objectives identified initially were:

- Improve and maintain water quality and preferred aquatic food resources so as to restore lakes Christina and Anka as important fall staging areas for waterfowl.
- Determine appropriate fish management programs for each of the three lakes.
- Consider alternatives for reduction of rough fish populations.
  - The need for better water level management to permit periodic draw-down to enhance control of rough fish and growth of aquatic plants and invertebrate populations in lakes Christina and Anka
  - The need for better understanding of the hydrologic budgets for these lakes.
  - The need for updating lake management plans to address current problems in further detail.

The Minnesota Department of Natural Resources (MNDNR) reactivated the Lake Christina Work Group to better address these needs and invited the CIA Lake Association to participate. At the same time the Lake Association began holding annual fundraisers in 2001 to provide an additional funding source to help support the cost of identified projects. The funds raised through these annual events ($17,000 – $25,000 net per year), and other special contributions by hunting clubs, other land owners and members helped encourage greater participation by MNDNR, Ducks Unlimited (DU), and other local organizations.

Jon Schneider, local DU staff member, has been able to provide valuable program guidance and technical assistance. This network of partners enabled all interested parties to carry out the necessary biological investigations, engineering services, more intensive water level management on tributaries, rough fish control operations and more specific planning for the future.

Among the major accomplishments to date, I would highlight the following:

- Establishment of procedures and equipment for recording annual precipitation systematic recording of water levels, sampling for water quality, fish population surveys and continuation of vegetative surveys in lakes Christina and Anka.
- Comprehensive review of hydrological data available for Lake Christina and development of a hydrologic budget by the U. S. Geological Survey.
- Engineering design and construction of new water control structures and fish barriers on Nycklemoe Creek and Lake Ina, with major assistance from DU.
- Removal of earth barrier on marsh adjacent to Lake Ina to enhance game fish spawning. (CIA Lake Association)
- Replacement of water control structure on the Elmer wetland to improve rough fish control for that tributary. (USFWS)

- Aerial application of rotenone for fish control in lakes Christina and Anka during October 2003. (Primarily MNDNR, DU and CIA)
- Continued research and monitoring to measure response of fish and vegetation to fish control operations on lakes Christina and Anka. (MNDNR, NDSU)
- Limited rough fish removal and stocking of walleyes in Lake Ina. (CIA)
- Further investigations by the Houston Engineering Company to determine alternative methods for lowering water levels in Lake Christina. (CIA, MNDNR, DU)
- Discussion with Pelican Lake Association regarding future water level management alternatives for the entire system. (CIA, MNDNR)

A lot has happened the past seven years, much of which likely would not have been possible without the presence and cooperation of the CIA Lake Association. The Lake Association has provided a medium for greater citizen input and interagency/conservation organization involvement to plan and conduct the projects completed to date. It also has provided another conduit for cooperative funding and in-kind support that probably is approaching more than $2 million to date. A special thanks to MNDNR and DU staff, participating hunting club owners and the CIA Board and members, who have worked so hard to make all this happen. Continuation of such cooperative efforts can and will accomplish even more during the years ahead.

The key question now is whether the aquatic food resources in lakes Christina and Anka come back and will the ducks return? During 2007, the water in Christina remained clear, the density of submerged aquatic vegetation continued to become denser with an increase in sago pondweed noted, muskgrass is apparently increasing throughout the bottom of the lake, and emergent vegetation is doing reasonably well in spite of relatively high water levels. The fall use by coots peaked at about 300,000 and a gradual increase observed for canvasbacks, redheads, ring-necked ducks, and bluebills (scaup), but not yet to the levels anticipated, based on response to previous rough fish eradication treatments. Reports indicate that a few carp, buffalo fish and substantial numbers of black bullheads are still present. A winter fish kill would certainly help. On the negative side, the water quality and aquatic food resources in Lake Anka seem to be deteriorating. This should be investigated further in 2008. Apparently there is an abundant carp population in Lake Ina that bears watching, but fortunately the new fish barrier is in place. Continued monitoring of all these aspects will always be required.

Harvey's favorite duck recipe!

Baked Duck – High Heat Method

By Harvey K. Nelson

1 duck – well cleaned and rinsed
1/4 cup lemon juice
1/4 cup Worcestershire
1 apple - tart
1 medium onion – chopped
1/2 cup prepared dressing if desired for larger ducks
salt and pepper

Mix lemon juice and Worcestershire; brush on duck, inside and outside until well coated. Salt and pepper to your taste. Stuff with equal amounts of onion and apple, and other dressing if desired. Place duck in baking dish on rack and bake at 575F. Small ducks require 15-20 minutes; medium size 20-25 minutes; large 25+ minutes. Experiment with timing to get desired texture, but watch carefully.

Baste with juices before serving. Try it, you'll like it; and it's fast!

[Modified from MWA, Wild Birds in the Kitchen]

LAKE CHRISTINA COOKBOOK

Chapter 2
Canvasback
The King of Ducks

Christina, Canvasbacks, Other Ducks and DU's Living Lakes Initiative

Jon Schneider, Manager – Minnesota Conservation Programs Ducks Unlimited, Inc.

"Canvasback, King of Ducks" – that phrase conjures up images of a regal duck species flying or floating on the water, and for some folks, of memorable duck shoots on big marshes such as Christina. For me, the canvasback is a very special bird because it is the first duck I harvested – a bull can in a November snow storm while shooting from a boat blind with my father and black lab at the age of 12 in Long Point Bay on Lake Erie's north shore, in Ontario, Canada. That duck, along with many other experiences with my Dad and dog at Long Point in the late 1970s and early 1980s watching and shooting ducks as they migrated south from Canada to Chesapeake Bay, is what motivated me to be a wildlife biologist and work for Ducks Unlimited (DU). That path led me to study at the Delta Waterfowl & Wetlands Research Station in Canada where I had the privilege of assisting research on canvasbacks in the prairie parklands of Manitoba and Alberta as well as on Delta Marsh wetlands. Similarly, it is now a privilege to help improve and protect Lake Christina and other critical waterfowl migration marshes in Minnesota to benefit the "King of Ducks," redheads, and other ducks.

The knowledge and information that has been learned about canvasbacks and other ducks over the years is vast and can't be summarized adequately here. Nonetheless, some generalizations are worth mentioning as they help relate the importance of Lake Christina to canvasbacks, redheads, and other large diving ducks as they move through Minnesota each spring and fall.

First, despite their notoriety as important ducks among hunters and artists, there aren't nearly as many canvasbacks and redheads in the world as there are other duck species more commonly harvested by hunters. The continental breeding population of both canvasbacks and redheads is usually less than one million each, with canvasbacks historically averaging only about 550,000 breeding birds and redheads averaging slightly more at about 625,000. Comparatively, scaup (bluebill) numbers have historically averaged a breeding population of about 5-6 million since modern surveys began (although their numbers are declining in recent years) and ring-necked ducks are typically estimated to number about 1 million in recent years (although they are difficult to survey). This makes canvasbacks the least abundant of the common game ducks in North America – something to consider as we strive to optimize habitat and harvest strategies to maintain their populations. The breeding populations of both species is closely monitored and managed to ensure that their numbers remain viable.

Canvasbacks generally breed farther north than redheads and other related diving ducks (pochards), primarily nesting in the prairie parklands and boreal region of Canada and Alaska but sometimes as far north as the Arctic. Redheads are more of a southern prairie breeding species and nest primarily in larger prairie pothole marshes south of the forest, although their breeding range overlaps with canvasbacks in the prairie parklands. Historically, redheads were probably very abundant throughout the Minnesota prairies, whereas canvasbacks seem to prefer the parklands and adjacent semi-forested areas to the north.

CHAPTER 2

For both species, however, the core of their breeding grounds is the prairie parklands of Manitoba, Saskatchewan, and Alberta. The highest density of breeding cans can be found in southwestern Manitoba, with the potholes around Minnedosa exceeding 10 pairs of cans per square mile according to annual waterfowl surveys, and annually accounts for about 10% of the total continental breeding population of canvasbacks. These parkland wetlands are also heavily used by breeding redhead ducks, which are closely related to canvasbacks evolutionarily and similarly nest over water in emergent aquatic vegetation such as bulrush or cattail, often on floating mats of vegetation. Here, canvasbacks and redheads often use and compete for the same wetland breeding areas. Unfortunately for canvasbacks, redheads often parasitize the nests of canvasbacks by laying their eggs in canvasback nests, while later also making a nest of their own.

Redheads have been documented to parasitize over 50% of canvasback nests, especially on large marshes where canvasback breeding activity is more conspicuous to redheads and breeding areas are shared. Thus, canvasback broods often contain one or more redhead ducklings. Canvasbacks are more likely to return to their natal breeding sites than other ducks, and are less apt to nest during their first year. Canvasbacks are relatively longed-lived, however, and their low reproductive productivity in early years is thought to be made up by years of reproduction later in their life. Reports of canvasbacks banded more than 10 years prior to harvest are not uncommon, with some reports of 18 and 20 year old birds taken – a long life for a duck!

Canvasbacks winter largely on either the Atlantic or Pacific coasts, depending on their origin, with smaller numbers found on the Great Lakes, Mississippi River, Gulf of Mexico, and other large inland bodies of water such as marshes in Florida, Louisiana, and Mexico. While their ultimate major winter destinations have remained very predictable over the years, it is their migration route and timing that has become legendary. Whereas some parkland birds and many birds from Alberta and Alaska winter along the California coast in the Pacific Flyway, the bulk of the continental population is thought to migrate through shallow lakes and large wetlands of the Dakotas, Minnesota, and Iowa to large pools on the Mississippi River near La Crosse, Wisconsin and Keokuk, Iowa. In Minnesota, key migration marshes for canvasbacks include Lake Christina in central Minnesota and Heron Lake in southern Minnesota. From the pools on the Mississippi, most birds appear to cross the lower Great Lakes enroute to Chesapeake Bay in the Atlantic Flyway, with fewer birds venturing to more southern marshes or remaining on the river. In contrast, large numbers of redheads also move south through Minnesota and the Dakotas in fall, but nearly all of them go on to winter directly south on the Laguna Madre along the Texas Gulf Coast.

The timing of this Midwestern fall movement of canvasbacks is very predictable, with most birds moving to the Mississippi River pools in late October and then onward to their final destination in late November or December before the river pools freeze. So predictable is their movement to the Mississippi River pools in late October, regardless of weather, that canvasbacks are often referred to as "calendar ducks" by hunters. In spring, migration routes are generally reversed, with many of those important stopover sites visited again in April. Most canvasbacks are back on their prairie and parkland breeding grounds by early May. Traditional timing and use of staging areas typify canvasbacks during migration. Canvasbacks are the fastest flying of the larger duck species, and appear equal to the speediest of the smaller ducks.

Canvasbacks appear to be flexible in their diet, with the ability to eat both plant and animal matter and forage in a wide range of water depths. Although canvasbacks appear to prefer aquatic plant foods such as sago pondweed tubers and seeds, wild celery, and duck potato, they quite readily consume other animal foods such as fingernail clams, snails, and other aquatic invertebrates when those prey items are abundant and/or when their preferred plant foods are in short supply. In contrast, redheads are nearly always found eating plant material, and generally prefer to forage in more shallow wetlands – sometimes without diving at all. Muskgrass (Chara sp.) is a common food of redheads in Minnesota.

Canvasbacks and most other duck species rely on healthy wetlands with abundant aquatic plant resources throughout their life cycle. This is especially true for canvasbacks and other large diving ducks during migration through Minnesota, however, given their long flights from northern Canada to the Mississippi River and east to the Atlantic coast or southern coastal marshes, and back again in spring. When food resources are abundant on fall staging areas such as Lake Christina, duck use rises dramatically – especially when prairie wetlands to the west are dry. In those years, such as 1990 when over 100,000 canvasbacks were counted on Lake Christina (approximately 10-20% of the continental canvasback population), quality habitat in key migration marshes appears to be biologically important.

Similarly, high quality spring migration habitat is thought to be important to large diving ducks such as canvasbacks and scaup that nest in the far north. Finding adequate food resources here during spring migration may be especially beneficial to the reproductive potential of large diving ducks that breed in northern boreal forest wetlands, which are not as productive as prairie pothole wetlands to the south. Diving ducks must forage in wetlands during spring migration to maintain body condition and enhance egg development prior to reaching their northern breeding grounds, or risk spending more valuable time doing so upon arrival up north. Some researchers have hypothesized that lack of quality spring migration habitat with abundant aquatic foods may limit spring body condition of female lesser scaup (bluebills) to the detriment of their reproductive potential and possibly their survival, which is very concerning given the apparent decline in the estimate of their breeding population in recent years.

To address these concerns, DU biologists refined the delivery of our conservation work in Minnesota and Iowa in 2004 to strategically focus on improving and protecting shallow lakes and large migration marshes for diving ducks such as canvasbacks, redheads, ring-necked ducks, and lesser scaup. Through our "Living Lakes Initiative" and in partnership with state and federal wildlife conservation agencies, DU established a goal of improving and protecting 400 shallow lakes and large marshes over 10 years for future generations of both ducks and people alike. These lakes will include many wild rice lakes in the forested region of Minnesota, key shallow lakes in the forest-prairie transition of Minnesota such as Lakes Christina and adjacent Lake Anka, and managed shallow lakes and large marshes down through the prairie region of southern Minnesota and Iowa.

The key to improving shallow lakes and large marshes is the ability to manage water levels and minimize undesirable fish populations, such as carp and black bullheads. By temporarily lowering water levels to help encourage natural winterkill of harmful fish in these shallow lakes and marshes, managers can improve water quality and maximize aquatic food resources in shallow lake systems like Christina. Once restored to a healthy clear water state with abundant aquatic plants and invertebrates, shallow lake shorelines and lands in their immediate

CHAPTER 2

watersheds must be restored and protected from further development through voluntary programs such as conservation easements and cooperative, conservation-minded private landowners.

Although it is expensive to engineer and install water control structures, fish barriers, and pumping systems needed to manage water levels, and equally expensive to secure land use rights on any lakeshore these days, DU and our partners such as the Minnesota DNR, U.S. Fish & Wildlife Service, and the Christina-Ina-Anka Lake Association can be successful – one lake at a time. For Christina and Anka, we are very close to long-term success on behalf of the ducks. Your purchase of this cookbook and support for our cooperative partnership work to improve Lake Christina is appreciated!

Lake Christina Cookbook

Hand carved Canvasback decoys, illustration by John House

Chapter 3
Rich Hunting Traditions in the Prairie Pot Hole Region – 1880s

The hunting traditions of the Ashby Minnesota, Lake Christina area can be traced back to the late 1800s. Ashby was like many emerging towns, primarily springing up due to the needs of producing grain, corn and other crops headed for the larger major cities. Few roads were available and the location of the railroad was the connective tissue for many struggling towns in west central Minnesota. On April 15th 1880, Knute Melby wrote a letter to the railroad magnate James J. Hill. He wrote to Hill on the difficulties he and others were having in trying to establish the original village (Ashby) on the land Knute Melby platted in 1879.

> "Dear Sir,
> We are laboring under a very great disadvantage in starting of our village by not having a Depot. People came here that would buy and build, but it is reported to many that no Depot building will be built here. If you would make a commencement, we would be well pleased."

Sometime in June or August a railroad Depot was finally built after encouragement and letters from many of the local people. The station Depot was located and called "The station at Pelican Lake," one of many built by the railroad called St.P.M&M Railway (St.Paul, Minneapolis and Manitoba Railways).

The narrow strip of land between Christina and Pelican Lake was the route for the railroad that began Ashby on its way to being a viable town. In the fall of 1882 the first hotel was built by Norman W. Kittson, the associate controller and business associate of James J. Hill. By now, both men were elderly and had less to do with the day-to-day operations of running a railroad. Thus, they had more time to spend on their enjoyment of hunting and fishing.

Prior to the hotel being built, Kittson and Hill would have their private rail car brought up to the area for lodging when they hunted. The hotel was built at the urging of Oliver Hawkins, a wealthy local businessman.

The story goes like this. Hawkins pestered Kittson over and over again until one day Hawkins suggested a card game. If he won, Kittson would build the hotel. If he lost, he would never mention again anything of a hotel. Hawkins felt that a hotel would be very beneficial for both commerce and sportsmen because hunting and fishing were becoming popular in the area.

The card game was played. Hawkins won and the hotel was built and finished by the fall of 1882 at a cost of over $20,000. Old documents and photographs showed the hotel as a large Victorian structure. It had between 40 and 50 rooms and the accoutrements were pretty spectacular for the day.

KITTSON HOTEL (Carl M. Iverson)

The hotel rooms rented for 50 cents. The furnishings were opulent for the day with wall-to-wall Brussels carpet, solid walnut furniture, marble topped dressers and

CHAPTER 3

wash stands, plate glass mirrors, expensive curtains and draperies on all windows and a kerosene lamp for lighting. The large dining room was equally elegant with bright shiny oak floors and large kerosene chandeliers hanging from the ceiling. The tables were covered with white linens and set with silver. There were two cooks, a pastry chef, dishwasher, dining room girls and chamber maids. There was also a bell boy who met passengers at the train station several times a day. It was reported that one of the many services offered included a lady of negotiable virtue who resided there for a time as well.

By Charles Broten & Carl M. Iverson
(Ashby, MN: The town that aspired to be a metropolis)

The railroad and hotel brought many a duck hunter from Minneapolis, St. Paul, Chicago and beyond to the famed fall duck hunting paradise called Lake Christina.

Hawkins was later quoted in a letter.

"Hotel Kittson, built last fall with money furnished by the public spirited "Commodore" whose name it bears, is a perfect gem; while it does not boast of its size it contains every modern convenience, and is elegantly furnished in the most thorough manner, and to the tourist, sportsman, commercial traveler or invalid it affords that rara avis, in the hotel world, a home."

Turn of the Century Duck Hunting
Edited from Grant County Herald,
"125 years of memories, 1879 – 2004"

Lake Christina was for years a magnet for hunters from far and near. The glory days of duck hunting live on in a select few Ashby, Minnesota residents who crossed the paths with hunters from all walks of life.

Picture the sky so full of ducks that the sunlight is filtered as though seen through heavy clouds. Picture a huge expanse of water, sun sparkling on waves that lap against rush beds, almost black with the presence of thousands of ducks. The picture is of Lake Christina, at the turn of the century.

The first settlers on the shores of Christina came there not only because of good farm land but also because of the plentiful game on the lake. Hans and Bendicta Palmquist were among the early settlers from Sweden settling on the south end of the lake in 1884. As Hans would do his daily chores in the barn located near the lakeshore, he would keep a loaded gun handy, and a sharp lookout through the open barn door. On many occasions Hans would be able to pause from milking the cows and bag seven to eight ducks with one shot!

Word of the 4,400 acre lake that was thick with ducks spread even in the late 1800s. In 1889 a man left St. Paul, Minnesota and headed for Christina, traveling by horse and buggy with two hunting dogs as companions. Sam Fertig was born in the 1860s, the son of Missourians transplanted to St. Paul. Nothing much is known about what he had done for a living before he arrived at Christina, but after his first trip here he decided to become a professional duck hunter.

CHAPTER 3

Sam hunted prairie chickens during his month long journey that first year, but arriving on the lake and seeing it so full of ducks and mud hens he decided to stay and hunt.

Sam went to Ashby, sold his horse and buggy and hunted all season. At the end of the first year he took the train back to St. Paul.

Sam Fertig made the Palmquist farm one of his bases for the next 35-40 years as he hunted on Christina. He would leave the cities in September and begin market hunting as soon as he arrived. Nels and Earnest Palmquist, sons of Hans remember helping Sam unload his duck boat one time, unloading 152 ducks, mostly redheads. He would take the ducks a few miles away to the railroad loading station near Ashby where they would be loaded in wood barrels and shipped off to Minneapolis and Chicago. At that time the going price for ducks was $3.50 a dozen for redheads and $4.00 a dozen for canvasbacks. There was no season and no limits in those early days on Lake Christina, so he quickly became known as one of the foremost hunters in the area.

Sam Fertig, First Market Hunter on Lake Christina

In 1889 Sam got married, and brought his new bride Mille to the Palmquist farm for their honeymoon. Millie's honeymoon cottage was a tent behind the barn. She had her biggest fright one day when Sam got stranded in a late season storm on an island out in the lake. No one knew where he was or if he was alive.

After the honeymoon hunt, Millie stayed in St. Paul while Sam continued to hunt. She eventually died there in 1978 at the age of 101.

The canvasbacks came to Lake Christina in huge numbers around the turn of the century, and with them the reputation of the lake was to grow as a prime hunting lake. By the 1920s and '30s to Sam's disgust, the well-to-do were claiming hunting rights on Christina, building up points from which to hunt and leasing lakeshore. It was in the '30s that Sam finally quit coming to Christina to hunt. One of Sam's proudest moments was having the honor of supplying the canvasbacks for a dinner in St .Paul for President Taft.

Sam's duck boat can be seen at the Elbow Lake Historical Center

Donated by Virgil Palmquist

Virgil Palmquist, 1943 with "Blackie" and his double barrel Ithaca 12 Ga.

Photo by Ethel Palmquist

HISTORIC HUNTING TRADITIONS AND THE REMAINING HUNTING CAMPS
The High/Low Pass, Palmquist property – 1880s

The high and low pass is located on the east side of Christina and separates Christina from Lake Anka. The high pass was originally owned by Wahlin (pro; walleen) The Wahlins owned that portion of the Sleepy Hollow not owned by the Virgil Palmquist family. Mr. Wahlin plotted and sold off 29 lots of various sizes in the late 1940s and early 1950s when there was huge interest in getting a piece of Christina hunting land. Seven cabins facing west from the east shore remain today. They include Gerlings, McPike, Hentges, Keckeson, Warnkes, Knudsen and Norby. Five cabins face east on Lake Anka; Kath, Holmberg, Soderman, Jacobsen, and Manley.

Ethel Palmquist, now 93 years old, has fond memories of her life on the homestead, about hunting, and of her family and many friends she made over the years.

Ethel, What can you tell me about your late husband Virgil? I mean, did he know Sam Fertig? Did he like to hunt?

"Oh, yes we new Sam, he was quite old when we got married in 1942, you know it was Virgil that pulled his old duck boat out of the barn cleaned it up and loaned it to the Elbow Lake Historical Center. Really, that old boat should be here on the farm, its part of the history of hunting Christina."

I've heard the stories of how many ducks were shot and shipped off to the big cities. Do you know anything about market hunting?

"Yes, you know, they stopped the train right at the Christina outlet so they could put the ducks on the train"

Ethel, I thought the depot was in Ashby?

"Yes, Yes it was, but they would stop, stop right there between Christina and Pelican Lake. They would see the team of horses with the wooden barrels full of ducks, and they would stop the train and load em right there!, they got real good money you know, the ducks, especially the canvasbacks were very popular in the Minneapolis restaurants."

Tell me about all the land the Palmquists owned, I mean where was it?

"Well, Hans and Bendicta were Virgil's great grandparents. They had two sons, Nels and Earnest. Nels was Virgil's dad and Earnest was Dwight's dad. Virgil got this farm, north of Melby and Dwight got the original homestead on the south side. The two farms were about 200 acres each and they both join each other. At one time most of the south and east side of the lake were part of the farm. We grazed cattle and grew crops here.

"During the depression, things were real tough here, there was no money, Virgil's dad sold off the pass to Wilson meat packing, he sold the low pass and the area by the duck slough to Mr. Strohmeyer from Duluth. He sold the big pass to Wilson for $1,000 dollars, it was a lot of money and it really helped out. Virgil loved the low pass, it was very important to him as he hunted there all his life. When we sold it they called it the St. Paul Pass," because all those people were from St. Paul, and they were all involved with the stockyards, either cattle or hogs. They were a rowdy bunch, I mean bottles were flying around those people all the time." They were nice enough to us, but they were real drinkers and partiers, they were!

CHAPTER 3

"I remember one time, Wilson and his crew were shooting a lot of ducks. They had so many that one of the fellows was going back to the cities, they gave him over 100 ducks to take back. He got as far as Sauk Center was pulled over and got fined by the DNR, it was a big fine!"

"Virgil got the opportunity to buy back the low pass or St.Paul pass, in the 1950s, and he did. We had to borrow money to do it, we had never borrowed money before, but it was so important to him to get it back." Isn't that where the Manleys hunt today? Yes we still lease it to Jake and Dave for $100 dollars a year!"

I heard that Virgil used to charge a dollar a car for hunters to pass through the farm and get to the lake, is that true?

"Yes we did for along time, but it got to be so many hunters coming through that it disturbed the cattle and just got to be too much, so we built the road, the one that goes down to "Sleepy Hollow" where all the hunting cabins are today."

Did Virgil like to hunt?

"Oh, yes, yes he did. He would hunt each day before school, shoot a few ducks and they would have them for supper at night.

"He had a real good friend from Melby, Bill Selander, they hunted all the time together. I remember one time Bill couldn't get his car started in Melby. So he jumped on the tractor and drove here to pick Virgil up at 4:30 in the morning, they both grabbed their guns and rode the tractor down to the lake."

What can you tell me about the High Pass?

"Well the pass, that piece of land connecting the Sleepy Hollow portion to the peninsula that goes out to the big pass was originally owned I think by Strohmeyer, he sold it to "Hood Norby" that's Howard Norby's father. Hood worked for the railroad in Evansville. In the old days, ducks would pass from Christina to Lake Anka, the hill was so high that they would shoot ducks as they crossed over."

Ethel are there any other stories or memories which stick out or you remember?

"Well did you know that we had a man stay here with us at the farm?" Well it was Judge W.A. Schultz from St. Paul. He had a wooden leg, he was pretty crippled up but he loved to hunt. I would make breakfast for him every day at 4:30AM, he would take that old little wood duck boat and load it himself in a truck, haul it down to the shore, and he would lay in that boat "ALL DAY LONG." "He always shot plenty of ducks! It was amazing to me he could do all that work, you know he was just so crippled up!

"There was also some pilots who hunted here, they would bring their wives with them, I know those ladies hated it here! They just didn't like it, they probably thought, 'What kind of women are you, living way out here in the country with no electricity, running water or bathroom.'

"We got electricity in 1947! It was so wonderful, WE COULD SEE, WE COULD ACTUALLY SEE!. We had to pay for the line all the way from Melby. Electricity changed our lives, we were so happy, it was wonderful!" Then came the well pump and we had running water too!

CHAPTER 3

"I hope the ducks come back, it used to be so much fun to go down to the shore and watch them swimming, flying and sitting there. Our world is just changing so fast now-a-days, I just miss seeing all those ducks. In the end, Virgil stopped hunting, it was about in the late 70s. He just wanted to see them, he didn't want to kill any more, he just watched them, and he died in 1985."

Ethel, Thank you so very much for seeing me and taking the time to share these stories.

"Oh, you're so welcome, make sure you get my picture of my Virgil, back to me!!"

Yes, ma'am, I will!

Greyhound Duck Camp / Douglas County Land Corporation – 1800s-1930s-2008

From excerpts taken from Minnesota Waterfowler Magazine and the comments of Duke Anderson, Guide and Caretaker

The original farmstead of the Andrew Nelson family of the late 1800s. Andy Nelson was a market hunter until 1918. Later he became the local Game Warden. During his market hunting days, he would drift or scull his sneak boat into a raft of cans and redheads. The ducks would swim in a tight ball ahead of him, and when the time was right he would lift his old black powder double barrel over the gunwales and fire both barrels into the flock. He would lay back down in the boat and remain still for a while until the cripples would quiet down. Then at the right time he would peek up over the boat side and shoot the cripples in the head with his 22 short. Then pick up all the ducks and head off for another raft of ducks. He would do this several times until he had sufficient numbers of ducks to prepare and place in barrels for shipment by the railroad.

Andy Nelson in the late 1930s with ducks from Lake Christina

Photo by Paul Englund

CHAPTER 3

In the early '30s, Andy had given up on the market hunting, paid more attention to his farm, and became a game warden.

One day on the job as a warden, Andy ran into some hunters and decided to check their licenses and limits. When he came up to them he could tell they were wealthy people, probably from the Twin Cities, Chicago or some important place. After checking them, the hunters asked if he knew of any good hunting spots they could try. Andy figured, they may pay well for a little "good" hunting and said, "I'll take you to the best damn dry land hunting spot on this lake if you pay for a guide fee."

That group of hunters included Eric Wickman, founder of Greyhound Bus Company and Alex Janes, chief counsel for the Great Northern Railway. They ended up hunting a lot with Andy. The early '30s were tough times in this country, especially for the small local farmers like Andy. Alex Janes found out Andy was about to lose his farm to the Federal Land Bank. They made him an offer to pay off his mortgage and other bills for the right to have exclusive hunting rights on all the property and the ability to build a lodge. Andy would be their guide, maintain the camp and ready the boats, decoys and blinds each fall. There were many great spots to hunt on that portion of the lake, but the best two were the "Point" and the "Pool." Both are still unbelievable late fall duck hunting spots today!

During that time, Frank Englund and his brother were both cooks on the "Empire Builder," the passenger train of the Great Northern Railway that ran from Chicago to Seattle. They had heard that the Greyhound Duck Camp was interested in obtaining chefs for the camp and possibly guides. Frank's brother became the chef and Frank was a helper and guide.

In 1956 many of the original members were aging and they sold out to John Hollern, C. Palmer Jaffrey (Pieper-Jaffrey), Conley

Brooks Sr. (Lumber), Harold Sweat (Honeywell), Sheldon Brooks (Minnetonka Boat Works), Bill Baker (IDS Tower) Donald Dayton (Dayton's Mercantile and Target stores), Ray Plank (Apache Corp & Foshay Tower), and Eddy Howard of Pieper Jaffrey. The name changed to Douglas County Land Corporation. By now these hunters had amassed 400 acres and approximately four miles of prime hunting lakeshore on the famed Christina. The new group found a local young man, "Duke" Anderson, to be their guide and camp manager, .

Duke Anderson 2008, 50 year Guide on Lake Christina

Duke, we have been friends a long time, and you've told me many stories about Christina and the history of your tenure here at the camp. We've hunted ducks and deer together, fished together, worked hard on the lake association and yes, you me and Rob have partied together! But we have never sat down with a pen and paper and recorded anything. I think today would be a good day to finally put something down, before it's too late, you know, for the cookbook. Tell me about the heyday of hunting Lake Christina.

CHAPTER 3

"When I started it was still the heyday of hunting ducks on Christina. Back then we shot only cans and reds. There wasn't any reason to shoot ringbills, bluebills or mallards. It wasn't **if** you would get your limit, it was when! No one was ever too worried about getting their ducks. The camp members here, for as long as I've been here, were pretty good hunters, in that they didn't take over their limit, they were pretty good that way. Some could really shoot and were avid hunters with good dogs, and others, well, they never could hit anything and their dogs weren't much better. We've made do, it's been fun and I wouldn't have changed anything. I've met a lot of nice and important people over the years, that if I wasn't here I never would have had the opportunity, so it has been good.

"In the early 1960s there was a duck epidemic which seriously dropped all duck numbers in Minnesota. The limit went to two ducks a day, some of the old guys got pretty disturbed and really limited their visits. During that time, I remember sitting in the big old game room, it's not a game room like you have today in the nicer homes, it was just our area near the fireplace where for as long as I can remember, sat that beautiful old oak octagon card table with the now worn green felt.

"I've watched a lot of fortunes get passed back and forth on that poker table! Anyhow, I remember sitting there one day with Palmer Jaffrey and Tom Crosby. The duck hunting was poor due to the epidemic. Palmer told Tom, 'Don't worry, Tom, give it a couple years and they'll be back.' And of course he was right. The divers did come back in full."

What about some of your memories as a guide for 50 years?
"Memories. There are so many to tell. One which is interesting and pretty funny is old Charlie Moore. He worked for Palmer Jaffrey. Palmer seemed to be connected to everything in those days. He even could call up the railroad, the Northern Pacific, and tell them hey, "put Charlie on the train up to Ashby" and a day later I would drive to Ashby and pick up old Charlie. Charlie was a big black guy about 250 pounds. He was a hell of a chef and a really good person.

"We were friends, as he didn't drive and I was the guide, during the middle of the day if he needed groceries it was my job to take Charlie into town and help him get the groceries. One time we were in the old Evansville grocery. Back then it was those real narrow aisles and shelves went up real high packed from floor to ceiling with dry goods and can goods.

"Charlie would get his cart and meander through the aisles with me walking behind. He was so big that he took up the whole narrow aisle. This one time, this big, black giant of a man came around the end of an aisle and he ran right up to this little old farm lady coming from the other direction. The expression on her face was utter fear; I mean she looked scared to death. I'm sure she had never seen a black person face to face ever before.

"I'd take Charlie to Ashby, too. Eventually he quit going to the stores. He got tired of the kids all staring at him, he was very self conscious of this and it bothered him.

"As big as he was, I've never seen a man so afraid of mice and the other little animals which always got inside the cabin somehow. On more than one occasion I'd come into the kitchen area and there was Big Old Charlie standing on top of a chair in the kitchen afraid of the mouse that just ran by.

"Man was he a good cook! He cooked everything right there in the kitchen, never on the grill outdoors. He could make anything. I remember we ate a lot of lamb in those days. Still today, his scrambled eggs are the best I've ever eaten.

"Charlie didn't like dogs too much either. Bill Gregory, the gentleman member who owned race horses and a big grainery in the cities, had a dog named "'Vigger'.

"He was up one time with his dog, Vigger. Old Mr. Gregory yelled at his dog a lot It really wasn't that good of a dog, but like most people it was his dog and to him it was good. Well, he'd yell at the top of his voice for Vigger to come, "VIGGER COME!" Every time he would.

"Charlie, one time confided in me and said, 'I wish he'd, Mr. Gregory would not come, not come to hunt, or at least not bring his dog.'

Duke, can you remember any other unique dog stories?

"That group of guys I was just talking about was starting to get old now and newer members were beginning to show up. About that time I did get two new dogs. I got them from Armstrong Ranch. Actually I was laying block in the cities; this other laborer knew I hunted Christina and that I was a guide there. He came up to me and said, 'I'll give you two really good duck dogs for a chance to come hunt Christina, one time'. I named the two black lab dogs Rowan & Martin, a male and female.

"That was during about the same time as that comedy show that was so popular— 'Rowan and Martin's Laugh In.' A few years later, the real Dan Rowan came to hunt here as a guest. I always let Rowan hunt with Rowan.

"The next year Dan Rowan came back and hunted again. I remember my Rowan sitting next to him in the lodge, right next to him with his drink planted squarely on top of my dog's head. He had this huge big black lab head with a big flat spot on top. It was perfect for sitting a drink there, and he wouldn't move til you let him.

"Dave Yager became a member. He was in charge of Federal Cartridge in Anoka. He, Dan Rowan and Tom Glead from Seattle hunted a lot together."

Who was Tom Glead?

"Oh, he was Chairman of the Board of United Airlines. That group came up for, for three or four straight years in a row. They were extremely good hunters and terrific shots. Tom Glead had a bad leg. I'm not sure what it was, maybe polio, I'm not sure. Anyhow, he had this beautiful English style double barrel Purdy, I mean the real fancy kind, and he would not only shoot with it, he used it as a crutch for walking. It was a real beautiful gun."

Anyone else interesting ever come up, I mean famous people?

"Ya, Bob Allison of the Twins baseball team came up here a lot."

Yes, he was one of my favorites, Duke. Number 4, I think?

"Yup you're right; boy could he throw that ball from right field in on a line to third.

That was before Doc Michienzi purchased the Twins Camp on the other side of the lake. Once he did, Bob

CHAPTER 3

spent more time hunting the rushes, with Doc, Billy Martin and that whole gang of baseball players.

"One time Bob Allison was sitting on the couch taking it easy. Two of our guys thought they'd be funny and with one on each end they hoisted this big old oak log into the cabin and set it down on Alison's lap. They thought they'd trap him there for a while. Bob just put his big ol' hands underneath that log, stood up and carried it back outside. He was a big, strong man!"

Anyone else?

"Chuck Vanderveer, the founder of Green Giant hunted here quite a few times. He was quite a guy; boy did he love to hunt. He owned a lot of land down in LeSeuer, but he came up here and hunted with his buddy Jaffrey.

"Jaffrey stopped hunting in 1968. I still remember that last weekend. He came up in the fall of '68. He never brought his gun, he sat around a lot, spent the whole weekend, and he was quiet. Never hunted, just sat there. He left on Sunday and I never saw him again!"

Well Duke, I'm getting a little full, I think this interview has to be postponed until next time. Any last comments?

"There's a big concern now, with all our new members, about the future of ducks and hunting. Ready to go?"

Yup, let's go.

(This interview was conducted at Millerville Liquor & Bar from 3:30 – 6:45 pm on February 21, 2008)

Duke Anderson started working for these business people as a guide in 1958. He was a local farm boy of 21 years of age, knew the lake well, was a crack shot and outdoorsman. During the off season he traveled to Minneapolis/ St. Paul and was a brick and concrete mason. Duke and his wife, Jan, are still the caretakers with his son and crack shot duck guide Rob Anderson. Rob, who is color blind, is one of the best duck identifiers I've ever hunted with. He does it by size, wing speed, flock size or pattern, shape and B&W shade for hen or drake! It's unbelievable to hunt with him as he only misses once every couple years, and that's after he lets you shoot first.

One time, during the very end of the season, while hunting with Rob, he said, "OK here come 25 bluebills busting around the corner. Remember, we can only take two for our limit and make em both drakes."

I shot and missed. He shot the two remaining ducks for the limit. Yes, they were both drakes!

November 2007
Duke & Rob Anderson out for a last hunt before freeze-up

CHAPTER 3

Whitney Camps on Pelican Lake and Lake Christina – 1890s

Robert Glen Anderson, a doctor from Minneapolis, purchased property on Pelican Lake, the downstream lake connected to Christina. In 1898 Carl Peterson — a local resident, market hunter and guide — was hired by Doctor Anderson to pursue his passion for duck hunting.

The hunting camp building was the original Ashby train depot moved to the Pelican Lake property sometime after the end of its usefulness for the railroad. Anderson and Peterson hunted together for many years until their deaths in or about the late 1940s. During their time hunting together, they amassed quite a few good hunting spots in the area. Their property and leases included Melby Lake, Little Lake, the Pelican property, the Christina lease and the Tresberg point on Pelican Lake.

Mrs. Helen Anderson, an avid outdoors woman and duck hunter, was very specific in her demands to relinquish the property for sale. She would only sell the land with the stipulation that she have the right to hunt every October 11th and 12th on either the Pelican Lake property or their lease on Christina owned by Joe Gradin. She was a noted writer and environmentalist who earned the honor of being called "The Grass Lady." She wrote the book, "*The Key to Grasses of Minnesota, Found in the Wild.*" This book was used for many years as a text book at the University of Minnesota.

In 1948 the camp was purchased by Mr. Valentine Wurtele, of the Valspar paint company of Minneapolis. The original members were Harry C Piper, George P. Clifford Jr., Charles R. Fowler, all Minneapolis business people and two gentlemen from Chicago associated with Sears Mercantile, Mr. George Harsh and Joseph F. Ringland. They were later joined by George Pillsbury, (Pillsbury Corporation) Steve Duffy (Hardware chain), George

West, Dick Vaughn (Valspar Paint Company) and Barney Clifford (Cream of Wheat).

Original rules for the camp stipulated that a maximum of only two women could be in camp at any one time.

The camp has had many cooks over the years.
- Sharky Westrin, the original Chef
- Donavin Grover (Postmaster of Ashby) served in the 1950s
- Kendora Peterson cooked in the '60s - '70s
- Colleen Jaenisch during 1970-75
- Wanda Risbrudt & Norm Hoff from 1980 to 2003
- Gwen Lillemon, 2004 to present

The guides were
- Carl Peterson, original
- Chris Peterson, 1958-1992
- Today, Greg Lillemon helps out with the blinds and decoys as well as readying the camp for each fall on Christina

Current camp members are Kim Whitney, Wheelock Whitney, Ben Whitney, David Whitney and Andy Andrews. Kim Whitney, the affable and friendly guy all the locals like, has a penchant for smoking those big fat cigars. One time while hunting the Joe Gradin point on Christina, things were a little slow in terms of duck hunting, so Kim lit a big cigar while enjoying the crisp fall air and bright afternoon October sunlight. It's not sure as to exactly what happened, but some have said that Kim got too relaxed, fell asleep and started the duck blind on fire with that big old torch he was enjoying.

Many local hunters have always referred to the famous point on the northwest side of Christina as Saylor's Point. The land and original homestead of John Gradin (1926), then his son, John

CHAPTER 3

Gradin Jr. and his son, Joe Gradin. The property includes 350 acres and 1.2 miles of lakeshore on Christina. The property is owned by Greg and Gwen (Gradin) Lillemon. Recently, a document was found that explains the story of that most famous duck spot, Saylor's Point.

> "He (Joe Gradin) said he remembered as a boy that his father had allowed public hunters to shoot off his two points. One year, however, he got disgusted with the litter and carelessness of the hunters and decided to preclude them and only allow a gentleman from Chicago to hunt there instead. This gentleman was Mr. Saylor, Joe said. He had a Negro chauffeur and another Negro assistant along just to open the farm gates as they crossed the property. He only came once a year, for many years. That's why the point has been called Saylor's, all these years."

Original Guide, Carl Peterson, mid 1920s

Millionaire's Point – 1917

The name given to the man-made point 100 yards in length that extends from the southwest side of Lake Christina. This was the name given by the locals back in the year 1919.

The owners were of the famed Archer Daniels Midland Corporation. Schreve Archer, his associates and their heirs, the Mairs family, owned the 13 acre property from 1917-1994. They sold to the second owners Brad & Teri Gruss who were very fortunate to meet (by chance) Joe Knutson of Ashby, who had been the last of many caretakers over the years. Joe knew everyone in town and a lot of people who would have wanted Millionaire's Point if they knew it was for sale. For some reason he took a liking to Brad and introduced him to the Mairs family of White Bear Lake. The Gruss family purchased the historic property, remodeled the ancient cabin in a way to keep it rustic and in the spirit. They now live there year round.

Frank Seidel, original hunting guide

CHAPTER 3

Shreve Archer, first owner

The following is from Dorothy Williams 1921-2003

She (1921) and her sister Laura (1920) were born in that little hunting shack.

"This is a little history on the Archer Daniels Midland duck club in Ashby, Minnesota, on Lake Christina as told by my father, Ralph Williams (also known as Red), who was a cook, carpenter and jack of all trades. He was employed in the Archer home as a cook in St. Paul, Minnesota. The men from the Archer Daniel Midland Grain Exchange had heard of good duck hunting on Lake Christina. They came to Ashby to acquire a piece of land for a private duck club.

"They wanted a point out into the lake for a blind to shoot ducks from. On this property was a high gravel hill which they were able to establish had once been a point of land out into the lake and that the ice over the years had pushed it up back into the hill, so they were able to return it to the lake.

"In the winter of 1918-1919 my father was sent up to Ashby to do this with local farmers using horses and scrapers. It was built on top of the ice during the winter and when the ice went out in the spring, it sunk to the bottom of the lake.

Gravel on ice 1919

Red Williams original chef and caretaker

'During the summer of 1919 he built the club house. It was ready for duck hunting that fall. He built the beds, tables and cupboards.

CHAPTER 3

"Two of his children were born in this building, Laura in 1920 and Dorothy in 1921. The family also consisted of an older brother, Carl, and a younger brother, Wesley, who were born in Cumberland, Wisconsin. The family lived in the club house during the year. When the duck hunting started we would move into the small log cabin behind the club house. My father spent the winters cooking for the Archer family while we stayed in Ashby.

"We left Ashby for Big Falls, Minnesota in 1924 where my father also cooked and ran the logging camps. In 1929 the family moved to Canada. Our last visit there was in 1995 and everything pretty much looked the same."

Dorothy Williams Brannan - Emo, Ontario, Canada

Picture of original Archer cabin taken 1994, "Invitation to friends at the first, Gruss Fall hunting party."

Lindquist Pass – 1940s

The Lindquist pass lies between Christina and Lake Anka and extends to Lund's Bay. The property is 190 acres and 2.1 miles of lake shore on the three lakes, (Christina, Ina, and Anka)

The Original Edland's Farmstead

> "Alex Kronberg bought it around 1940. He owned it until 1953, when he sold it to my father Hubert Lindquist."

John, do you have any early memories about that time?
> "I still remember the first day I hunted the pass. Well actually, we didn't get to hunt it, we leased it to the 3M camp for many years, and we needed to do that to pay for the land."

How come your father got a chance to buy that precious land, John? I mean that's about the same time that many of the wealthy people from the cities were getting the best spots.
> "My dad, when he was young, say about 20-21 worked for Mr. Kronberg. He, Mr. Kronberg, was a foreman for U.S. Steel. They worked the iron ore boats in the Great Lakes. A lot of Lund Township boys ended up working there. It was good money and they liked the way those farm boys could work. Anyhow, my dad got to buy from Kronberg because Kronberg liked him. That was the only reason we got it."

What about that first hunt?
> "Well, I was 12 years old. I was the duck chaser for the 3M hunters. There were 10 of them that leased our land and they hunted there a lot during the season. I got paid $5 a day plus any shotgun shells I needed to shoot cripples. I thought I was pretty lucky, I mean, getting paid to go hunting on the pass! Anyhow, that first time of mine

CHAPTER 3

there the hunting was awful good and they were shooting a lot of redheads. There was so much action from all directions, (some flying from behind us from Lake Anka, crossing the pass on their way to big water of Christina and a whole lot more coming off Christina and going into Anka anyhow, with all the shooting one shot duck flew into the face of one of the hunters and knocked him pretty hard. He got a headache and had to leave early.

"Well, my Dad heard all the shooting and he came back down to the pass about 9:45 am. I heard him say 'Boys, you better count your birds.' Well they did and they had 70, mostly redheads; they were 20 over the limit!

So did you hunt a lot with your Dad? And how about your Uncle Roy?

"Yes we hunted quite a lot together, but since we leased the land, we hunted the three potholes on the property and got plenty of shooting all the time."

Hubert Lindquist, with ducks from days hunt.

What can you tell me about those early hunting days, I suppose the decoys were all wooden?

"Yes, they were all wood and they were heavy, but I remember when the first plastic ones came out. They were called "Victors." My Dad bought a dozen and boy I thought I'd gone to heaven when I got to pick those up after the day's hunt, back then."

John and his wife, Pat, bought the property from his sister at the passing of his father in 1979. They lived there part time from 1981 until they sold their house in Alexandria and then moved in full time in 2003.

John was one of the founders of the Lake Association. He has been the President of the CIA Board since the inception. It is because of his consistent work effort and fund raising abilities that we are where we are today. John and Pat were leaders in conservation as well. They were the first in Minnesota to sign up all of their property into the DUCKS UNLIMITED perpetual easement program. During my many discussions with John in and out of the fishing boat, duck blind and during pheasant hunting, one thing stands out — HE is a committed outdoorsman who has a passion for doing the right thing. John admits his hunting days will come to an end all too soon, but the passion will continue for many years on his property because of his action to secure that land in the DU easement program. I, like a lot of others too many to mention, are honored to be his friend and hunting companion.

Redheads flying over Lindquist Pass

CHAPTER 3

Wilson/Soderman's Pass

Anton Soderman, 1930s, with ducks Lake Anka in background

The Soderman family, beginning with Anton Soderman, had a cabin in the "Sleepy Hollow" area during the late 1940s. They hunted the open waters of Lake Christina, off Spoonbill Point or often rowing from the cabin location out into the bull rush stands of Christina. When not hunting the lake, they frequently would watch and listen to the thunderous reports of the shotguns exploding and ducks falling from the Wilson Pass, a view from their cabin location on Anka. During that time they had no idea that the famed Wilson Pass would be their's someday!

The Wilson Pass History

Approximately 11 acres at the very end of the peninsula which extends north of the "Low Pass," "High Pass," "Sleepy Hollow" area and Palmquist property was originally owned by the St. Paul, Minneapolis, and Manitoba Railway Company and later Northern Pacific Railroad Company. The land was tax forfeited and sold at private sale for taxes in 1902. But in 1915, the Palmquist brothers, Nels and Ernest, acquired the land. They sold it to Carl Engemoen in 1928.

Engemoen cleared the land at the tip of the point where the peninsula ended with only a narrow channel, connecting Christina and Lake Anka. Carl Engemoen hunted there with his son-in-law, Roy Wilson. After Engemoen died in 1937, Roy Wilson acquired the point in 1938. Thereafter it became known as "Wilson's Pass."

Wilson had professional pits made with sliding lids that protected the hunters seated below. He sat alone in an all steel pit (perhaps an old "sink box") that was dug into the ground close to the channel. Although the opposite side of the channel was not hunted until the late 1940s, Wilson had trouble sharing the ducks with his neighbor across the channel, Hubert Lindquist. It did not help matters that Wilson sat in the end pit with his right hand on his shotgun and his left hand on a bottle of Brooklyn Handicap. (In later years the bourbon gave way to Hudson's Bay Scotch.) One year, he strung barbed wire down the middle of the channel and told the boys across the channel that they could shoot at anything they wanted, but that if it fell on his side of the barbed wire, it was his duck and if it fell on their side, it was their duck!

Roy Wilson first sold the point for $100,000 in 1948. In 1952 he sold it again for $75,000. Each time the would-be buyers put down enough earnest money to be considered a lease payment, hunted there for a year or two and then failed to complete their purchase. With the decline of hunting on Lake Christina and closed seasons on canvasbacks and redheads, the property was not marketed. But in 1973, Roy Wilson fell while he was mowing his lawn and lost an eye. His hunting days were over and he had an odd reason for selling. His son and friends continued hunting his pass, but they did so laying on the ground next to the once-fancy pits. During that time the pits were used for empty beer can receptacles. Roy Wilson was determined to teach his son a lesson.

Don Soderman (Anton's son) made one offer $1,000 more than the asking price. Members of the 3M Board of Directors made an offer at the same time. Wilson accepted the Soderman's offer because he wanted to see Lake Christina remain unchanged. Strangely, he was an avid conservationist (at

CHAPTER 3

least in his speech) and did not want development, cabins or commercial hunting on Lake Christina.

At closing, Roy Wilson was asked for his greatest memory of duck hunting on Lake Christina. He smiled and said that it was an easy question. He answered:

> "It was the day the wardens hit us from three directions at once! We had 60 Reds stashed in the weeds and they never found one!"

It took three full boat loads to haul empty beer cans from the pits, and two more years of rebuilding pits, cutting trees and trimming weeds before the old pass was restored to its former glory by the Soderman family. It remains a private family hunting pass to this day.

Ron Schara would write a column in the *Minneapolis Star and Tribune* shortly after the Wilson Pass officially became "Soderman's Pass." About the famous Lake Christina duck passes, Schara wrote:

> "The ghosts of waterfowling are alive and well around Melby, Minnesota ... So choice are these natural flyways that confirmed duck hunters have paid thousands of dollars to own a barren piece of land containing nothing but spent shotgun shells."

Lake Christina Cookbook

Don Soderman with ducks, from the Soderman Pass, 1975

June Soderman with sons, Tom and Tony

CHAPTER 3

3M Camp – 1950s
Excerpts from the Grant County Herald and Gwen & Jim Risbrudt, Camp Chefs

This camp is still in operation today. The camp is located on the west side of the south side of the lake about three-quarters to one mile from the large bulrush stand. The property was originally owned by Sam Lee. During the late '50s, 3M CEO Clarence Sampair (Sam) started the camp as a getaway for executives and important customers of St. Paul's, Minnesota Mining and Manufacturing Co.

When originally opened, they had an excess of people there. The shooting of ducks was very liberal. Albert Hoff the original guide finally had enough and said,

"You can't be bringing so many people out here. The shooting is way too much and it's not good to bring this much attention to the west side. We either do something about it or find a new guide!"

Shortly thereafter, Sam decided that it would be best to only have select employees and build another place more focused for their important customers. That may be around the time they expanded "Wonewok," the famous fishing camp located on Big Mantrap Lake, north and east of Park Rapids.

Over the years, the 3M group obtained several hunting areas in and around the area. They hunted the Lindquist pass, Lake Formal near Dalton and other shallow lakes and potholes.

There is a long history of many locals who guided and served food to these business people from the Twin Cities.

At the age of 85, Albert still remembers his beginning days as a young boy hunting this area. His first gun purchased was a single shot H&R, Harrington and Richards, that cost $4.80. He began his guiding days in the 1930s when he helped Carl Peterson guide for a hunting party on Pelican Lake.

Albert's son, Glenn, guided the 3M people for many years. I had the opportunity to meet Glenn in 1994, shortly after purchasing Millionaire's Point.

Growing up as a young hunter, my father, Fremont, always taught me to find a good location with the wind at your back and to keep well covered and especially never, never, move anything but your eyes when the ducks were approaching. Hunting the west side of Christina is a whole different deal. When the wind is at your back like it's supposed to be, it pushes the diver ducks away from shore. Cans, ringbills, redheads and bluebills aren't much for flying over land the way it is, they prefer the big open water. But it is the sago, celery and fresh water shrimp that makes them a little dumber and more likely to decoy. Especially when the decoy's are right in the middle of that salad bar of sago. The first year on the point we had great difficulty in figuring out the wind and how to set the decoys. That fall I ventured over to the 3M camp and introduced myself. Glenn was there with several of the members. He stood out immediately from the rest, there was no guessing as to who the guide was. Glenn had that un-mistaken look of a guy who had spent many years outdoors in the wind and sun. He said, "Brad nice to meet you, next week sometime I'll stop by and talk to you about how to set out your decoys, and I'll show you why an east, southeast or northeast wind will bring those big cans right in to you." Glenn never made it over. He was killed that next week while working for the highway department on highway 78, the one that runs right by 3M on the west side of Christina.

Glenn's nephew, Steve Wick, took over as guide. Steve spent many years hunting alongside his father, uncle and even Albert. He is a great duck identifier and probably one of the quickest shots I've hunted with.

CHAPTER 3

Some of the more notable 3M hunters were Bob Tucker (legal), Dick Brust (accounting), Ray Herzog (CEO), Bill Aitkan (R&D), Erv Hansen (accounting), George Swenson, Dick Priebe and Tim Hoffman.

They have had the same cooks at their camp for the last 35 years. Gwenny and Jim Risbrudt of Ashby. Their favorite story refers to the fact that the original group just wanted to relax. "They enjoyed both shooting and watching the ducks. They never would go anywhere, they always stayed around the camp or went to their other leases," explained Gwen.

> "They also love to eat and after dinner they often would sing in camp. Many of the group loved to sing. In fact, Bob Tucker, Dick Priebe, Dick Brust and Herb Hanson sang together in a quartet! Many times during the good hunting around Halloween, they would invite the children of the cooks and helpers out to the camp. "Jimmy Crack Corn" was the song they loved to entertain the kids with. They would sing every verse. I didn't know there were so many verses to that song."

Some have said that in the days of low water and a healthy sago pondweed growth that the fall winds would push huge mats of floating sago into the shoreline. It was not uncommon for the floating bogs to stretch out over 75 yards from shore. It made hunting difficult to say the least. 3M had a point built which stretched out 30-40 yards from shore, but over the years the ice heaves have removed a great portion of the point. The current fall hunting guide is Steve Bjorklund, a recent resident of the area who owns the small farm adjacent to the 3M property.

The Twins Camp – 1950s

In 1952 Dr. L.J. Michienzi the Club physician of the Minnesota Twins, and Barney Browne the owner of a Minneapolis Ford dealership purchased a cabin and obtained a lease from the old Palmquist site on the south side of Lake Christina. They named their cabin the "Duck Inn." The location was very near to the massive bulrush stand on the south and southeast side of that historic lake. Back in those days, it was important to be located near the rushes as the ducks staged out in the middle of the lake would find refuge in every little pocket or opening between the thick bulrush beds. The hunting as they say, was fast and furious. When the lake was really healthy, the sago pondweed was so thick that you could not use any form of outboard motor. Hunters used long push poles and small duck boats to maneuver through the entanglement of vegetation. There are many stories of the rivalries that took place in trying to be the first one to that favorite spot.

At that time there were approximately six to eight shacks on the south side and 10-12 hunting shacks located at what's now called Sleepy Hollow, the spit of land that extends from the Melby village west and splits Lake Christina and Lake Anka by 50 -100 yards. More than one heated argument was had when two boats claimed the same hunting grounds. During the heat of the migration, many would push pole out at midnight with a kerosene lamp, sleeping bag, decoys and some old paper shotgun shells to claim their spot!

During the later years of Dr. Michienzi's stay, (1952 -1973) he became a real popular and favored hunter by many of the town folk. Anyone associated with the Twins was held in high esteem because of the popularity of baseball.

Guests that stayed at the Duck Inn were pretty notable; Calvin Griffith (Twins owner), Sherry Robertson, Bob Allison and the

CHAPTER 3

highly wound and excitable coach Billy Martin. There was another owner in that select group, Len "Gramps" Aves, who purchased the hunting spot from Doc and hunted Christina from 1955 through the mid '80s. Len Aves, like many hunters, kept a log. Included here are a few of the written remarks.

> November 2, 1955. "Lloyd Palmquist called yesterday and stated that he has never seen so many mallards flying on Lake Christina. This is apparently the migration! The temperature this morning is about 17 and the lake is freezing. We shot 55 ducks and picked up 36, having difficulty finding them in the strong wind."

The big mallard migration from Canada usually takes place after Christina freezes. These are the giant greenheads almost in full plumage you see landing in cornfields. Yes, it is cold hunting but rewarding.

> November 7, 1956. "Doc called Barney last night and told him that the snowstorm in North Dakota was finally moving into Minnesota. We arrived in the storm that had slowed our driving down to 20 mph. We listened to the election and went to bed happy that Eisenhower was still winning. This morning the winds are out of the NW at 45 mph with blowing snow. The ducks were coming into the decoys so fast that we took turns shooting and never had to wait longer than two minutes for a chance to shoot!"

> October 20, 1963. "The Minnesota Twins gang arrived again this year. Len Aves took Bob Allison and Doug Zimmerman out for an afternoon hunt. Billy Martin stayed on shore and was shooting Blackbirds after the close of the hunt. It wasn't soon after that Jim Meyers the game warden showed up as he thought we were shooting ducks after hours. Billy got a ticket anyhow."

Doc Michienzi sold out in 1972 and retired on Sewell Lake, north of Ashby. He wrote the following after the 1972 season.

> "The memories of ducks swimming in front of the old cabin will stay with us for many years. Years of hunting in the marsh out of boats, rigging blinds, picking up icy decoys in the late fall will be cherished as days of youth and determination and the love of an early fall chill warmed by a cup of alkali coffee. We are older now...We no longer hunt from sunrise to sunset...We do not change blinds and pick up our decoys three or four times a day. We are not determined to destroy our heritage but rather preserve it so others that will join us in future years will have the same internal fulfillment."

The current owner of the Twins camp is Mel Bois, an avid outdoorsman of 62 years and an overachiever in Ducks Unlimited.

Mel lets his friends stay at the "Duck Inn," whenever he can't be there. The current caretaker and guide is Kevin Fick. Located inside that cabin are old pictures, an ancient fireplace, some decoys and the old painted steel cupboards from the '50s. The white steel cupboards with the worn red plastic handles give off a cold feeling and a shiver when you look at them, but whenever you are there, the rest of the cabin gives off a warm cozy feeling and you just can't help but think of the conversations and craziness that must have surrounded Doc Michienzi, Billy Martin, and the rest of those characters when they escaped Minneapolis for a few days to enjoy the beauty of the duck marsh and Lake Christina.

The ducks are still swimming out in front each fall, in the bulrushes, just like they have since Doc's days in 1952.

Mel Bois must be the person Doc wrote of as he still has the burning desire to hunt the late fall, before freeze up.

CHAPTER 3

I've hunted a lot with Mel. I know he is mentally crushed each year when the lake freezes and the hunting is over. Mel is one of those few in Minnesota that would rather be freezing in the duck blind then freezing in the deer stand. Some of the best duck hunting is on opening weekend of deer hunting! When Christina typically freezes over, Mel moves his last few chances for bagging a bird in early November to Lake Vinge near Dalton, one of the last lakes to freeze because of its depth. He is a spirited, competitive hunter with a big warm heart, and an undying love of duck hunting!

"Sky" and Mel Bois, with late season bluebills.

Oxley/ Warnkes Camp – 1950s

Earl Oxley, the self proclaimed "Mayor of Lake Christina," was a self promoting character who loved company. He came from pretty famous roots, as his grandfather was a taxidermist and one of the early photographers of wildlife in Fergus Falls, Minnesota. There is a major hotel chain in Fergus Falls. Recently, the "Shallow Lakes Forum V," sponsored by Mankato University, MNDNR, Ducks Unlimited, USFWS and others, held a two-day learning and training symposium. Right there in the middle of all the meeting rooms is "The Oxley Room", named after Earl's famous grandfather and photographer.

As a young man, Earl started off in insurance. His boss owned the duck camp on Christina. Earl had a chance to visit and hunt the lake with his boss and customers. His first time hunting there, he explained to a companion, "I've never, never seen so many ducks in my life and have never had the opportunity to shoot like that before."

Sometime in the '50s, Earl's boss became very ill with some form of cancer. He said to Earl one day in the office, "Earl, I'm dying, and I won't give the duck camp to my damn wife or the kids. You're the only one I know who would enjoy it, so it's yours, if you want it."

Earl did inherit his boss' hunting rights and cabin on Lake Christina. He formed a group called Oxley's Hunting Camp, (for hire) which was a combination of his friends and business associates from Edina, Minnetonka and Minneapolis.

During my first visit to Christina, I became lost when trying to find that narrow partial gravel, mostly mud road from the village of Melby down to what is now called Sleepy Hollow, where I was to meet Mark Gerling and Tony Soderman for my first hunt on the famed lake. The road meanders through the Palmquist's sloughs and trees as it goes up and down over the little hills.

CHAPTER 3

As I was driving in, a red pickup truck with topper was going faster than any normal person would dare drive. It was coming toward me. Luckily I saw it on the second hill before it slipped under my view. I stopped, pulled over to the side as far as I could and waited three seconds before the red truck flew over the hill and slammed on the brakes while the dust and gravel exploded into a cloud around my old Jeep Wagoneer. The window was rolled down and this little old guy with a curmudgeon-like face said, "I'm Earl Oxley, who the hell are you, and what are you doing on this road?"

"Ah, sir, my name is Brad Gruss. I'm lost and looking for the Soderman hunting place."

"Well, Ok then, I guess it's all right. I'm Earl. I own the big red cabin on the hill. Just follow this road and take the first right." And he sped off!

Earl was a character and his braggadocios way of letting everyone know he was special (at least in his own mind) was amusing. Once you did get a chance to know him on his terms, he was indeed a pretty good old guy!

During those early years of hunting the lake on weekends in the fall, after the long drive on a Friday from Excelsior, I grew to love the area, and felt awfully excited and fortunate to know somebody who could give me access to this hunting paradise. During those years, I spent many nights sleeping in my truck after hunting and partying, but it was an opportunity in getting to know the rest of the hunting characters who really were fortunate to own a piece of Christina.

The Oxley camp was located on the east part of Lake Christina. The cabin was originally made from a railroad boxcar. Earl had added a bedroom addition and later a living room, bedroom and bathroom on the lower level. There were two double bunks in the bedroom addition, and one double and one single bunk (Earl's) on the lower level. The kitchen and eating area was in the former boxcar part of the cabin.

There were seven to ten members at various times. Members included, in addition to Earl Oxley:

Ed Hentges	Glenn Gausman
Ralph Goughner	Spencer M. Dean
Bob Ryder	Don Hanbury
Court Olsen	Jack Chandler
Steve Emerson	Roger Halvorson

The camp members hunted a lease Earl had on a large slough (South Jolly Ann) and a small lake (Rat Lake) on the Eldred Ness farm, which was about five miles north of Lake Christina, and on a point on Stockhausen Lake (owned by Spencer Dean and Ed Hentges).

Tom and Pam Warnke are the current owners. They are both awfully nice and are good caretakers of the lake. They have remodeled that old box car, but left the original car siding down as the floor in the kitchen! They are very active in the CIA and, they drive a lot slower than Earl!

Early canvasback decoys used on Christina

Chapter 4
Hunting the Rushes by Duck Boat
By John House

I grew up in a duck hunting family on the eastern side of Minnesota, hunting ponds and potholes for the "puddle ducks" that both breed and migrate through there in the fall. Diver ducks were unknown to us. However, in high school I met a gal (my future wife) who had strong family ties to a small town in western Minnesota called "Melby," a place I had never heard of. In the fall of 1972 a bunch of us headed northwest and arrived late at night to her vacated grandparents' home in Melby, which was also her mother's birthplace. The next morning I woke up and looked out the second story window upon the most beautiful rolling land, woods and water that I had ever seen in my young life. We spent the rest of the weekend just driving around and taking it all in, amazed at the pristine beauty of the area, and that included a swing around the large and magnificent Lake Christina. The road along the east end of the lake runs right along the shore for a stretch, giving the traveler a birds-eye view of that end of the lake. That weekend we saw something I had never witnessed before - huge groups of ducks simply rafting up in open water on this very large lake. The duck hunter in me went off like a roman candle – I couldn't believe my eyes. What was this place? I stood there on the east end drooling, my mind spinning. How I could possibly get closer to those ducks.

In 1977 I married Barb and in July '78 we moved into that house in Melby, our young lives before us and possessing not much more than youthful zeal and a duck hunter's heart. I figured out a way to gain legal access to that glorious east end that had left such an impression on me years earlier and I began to shoot ducks, but it was mostly luck. These were strange waters and strange ducks – I had had no experience regarding divers and it was a long road I had to travel to learn this new sport, for it was nothing like what I was used to. Big water, big waves, big decoy rigs and big ducks – and the diversity of birds! My son Tom's first duck hunt was on that east end when he was just shy of three years old,. I remember that shortly after the noon opener he had to take his nap, and he slept like a log on the bottom of the boat. The hunting was phenomenal in those days despite my ignorance, particularly for big Redheads. I had swallowed the hook deep and there would be no escaping the lure of this lake.

Eventually I was attracted to the large rush beds on the south and west ends of the lake, mostly because of the ability to hunt far out from shore. I started on the west end the same way I had hunted the east end – in a homemade duck boat powered only by a pair of oars. In those early years we put in on the north side of the creek leading out of Christina – there was no public access yet and it was a rocky trail leading down to the lake, with no ability to back a boat down to the shore. No matter, I was so poor that I didn't have a trailer anyway, we just threw the boat into the back of the station wagon and close enough was good enough. It was all bull work but those of you who have the same disease will acknowledge that it was a labor of love, for every hunt begins with hope and pure joy, and the labor involved is but minor necessary pain.

In the beginning we hunted not far out from the access, as rowing a wooden boat with a couple of hunters, a large Chesapeake retriever and many decoys is tough on a calm day, not to mention when the wind is blowing. Again, the learning curve bit deep for I had a lot to learn about hunting those rushes. But slowly I learned, at first with my own son and later with trusted friends, we learned the "ins and outs" of that end of the lake. We learned what different species like regarding decoy

CHAPTER 4

sets, the size of the openings they require, proximity to shore that they will "work," the times of the season that they are "in," how and when to call them, the type and style of blind to use, which weather is best for hunting, even which wind is best for which spot. You name it, we lived it those early years. How many mistakes we have made, both errors of commission and omission, but steadily we learned, and that's the important point.

The lake has been poisoned three times – 1965, 1987 and 2004, all of which have been successful for a time but inevitably the fish come back with a vengeance, easily within 10 years after the poisoning. We started hunting in the late 1970s, well after the '65 poisoning. To look at the lake in those days was to dismiss it out-of-hand, as the water color and clarity was so putrid green that it could be said without exaggeration that it somewhat resembled green paint. Migrating waterfowl would still stop in as the place must have still looked "ducky" from the air, but once on the lake they would soon discover that the salad bar was closed and there was little duck food to be found. Can you imagine beating your wings furiously for those many miles, then dropping down after a long night of flying with fresh food expectations, only to find a bare plate? You couldn't afford to hang around very long and they didn't either. They'd migrate in, find little food and quickly depart for better waters. Therefore, in those days, rarely did the public see any build-up of waterfowl on the lake, even though a public road affords very open views of the lake on three sides. If I had a nickel for every time I heard somebody back then tell me "well, there's no ducks on Christina." The dirty little secret was that if you were out there when the birds first arrived, you could have some of the greatest shooting you've ever had. And we did in those early days of "green paint." Sure, we bombed out sometimes but the good times made it all worthwhile.

Over the years I have been fortunate to become friends with some of the landowners around the lake, and even more fortunate to be invited to hunt from their points and passes. Which ones are better than others is a debate best held in the evening over adult beverages and fine cigars, and we've done plenty of that (the truth is, they're all good at times). But let me say this: there is something magical about being "out there," boat hunting far from shore. Man has been given five senses and they are well-fed when boat hunting the rushes - seeing the pre-dawn stars and then the dawn sky (be it clear or cloudy), birds working way out on the lake, the beauty of a flock cupped and committed and then a clean kill; hearing the roosted birds in the pre-dawn darkness, the waves lapping at your boat, the wind whistling (sometimes roaring) through the rushes and then flocks banking hard for your set of decoys, sounding much like jets; smelling the wind-driven water, the coffee mingled with cold, fresh air and the pre-dawn cigar, and the smell of freshly-burned gunpowder; feeling the rocking of the boat and the cold northwest wind, hopefully on the back of your neck and not your face; and tasting your wife's sandwiches, coffee or tea and the duck call that has sat in a cold clammy box since your last hunt. All of this is part of the boat hunting experience and it is a treasure for those of us with the incurable virus called duck hunting.

One of the drawbacks of hunting the rushes is the competition, although I must admit, I had a chance to visit with old-timer Bill Selander (Melby) about this before he passed on to his reward in his early '90s. I was whining about all of the other hunters I was dealing with out there and his answer surprised me. He said, "You haven't seen anything! Back in the '40s, you had to be at your chosen spot by midnight and spend the night in the boat if you wanted to keep it." That put me in my place and I haven't been so caustic about it since that talk. But at times it's trying, to be sure.

CHAPTER 4

There's what we call the "flashlight kings," guys who come out in the pre-dawn darkness with million-candle-power beams and they try to find their places by those lights. The simple fact is that you can see 100 times better with no lights at all, just invest a little time during daylight hours and familiarize yourself with prominent landmarks and line your spot up with them. You will be miles ahead that way, even in the morning darkness.

Then there's the late-comers: guys who come out at shooting time or even a little later and buzz through the rushes for their entire two mile length, only to find that all the decent spots are taken, at which point they start back to find a lesser spot somewhere, meaning they have hosed everybody along the way, both ways, and all of this usually during the first half-hour of shooting time, which is generally the best shooting of the day. Then in resignation they set up 80 yards from us or someone else, hosing someone yet again, this time in broad daylight. The reasons they come out late are many and varied, be it a good time the night before or the alarm didn't go off or maybe they don't want to fight the darkness; but it's so rude to the hunters that paid the price to secure their spot early.

One year there was a party that came out not in a duck boat, not a jon boat, not a bass boat, but a real live racer-style speedboat, like a cigarette boat you'd see in Miami. That boat was so huge and long and the long-shaft motor had at least 150 horses, probably a lot more. That alone was incredible, but he was also towing a duck boat behind him, with people in it. He had the power trim as high as it would go, and he went just outside our decoys spouting a rooster tail of mud and water at least 6' high, and I have the pictures to prove it (we never saw him again). Sometimes we've had flocks working our decoys and another party somewhere down the line has an opportunity for a shot and so they let go, spooking the birds that were working our blocks. This is nobody's fault, it's just a hazard of hunting public water and you have to accept it as it is.

One morning I took my uncle and his young son out real early so as to secure our spot. I mean real early. Then we anchored in the strong winds and we actually curled up and fell asleep as we bobbed in the big waves. Until it started raining, that is. By the time light dawned, these guys were so fed up with the cold, windy and wet morning that they were "done in" before they had fired a shot. We shot a few ducks but it wasn't the best morning for shooting, the birds just weren't there. We were cold to the core, and when that happens, a warm room isn't enough to warm you up. When you get back you need to soak in a tub of hot water for quite awhile to get your core temperature back up. So I ran a tub for my cousin, but I had forgotten to load the softener with salt so it was hard, rusty water that he climbed into. Needless to say, the whole morning was too much and he hasn't been back since. I still feel kind of bad about that one.

We have been blown off the lake three times in 30 years, meaning the winds came up so fiercely that we had to run for our lives and leave the decoys behind, retrieving them the next day after the winds subsided. One of those times started as a normal hunt with a mild south wind, with sporadic shooting. But around 11 am the south wind went dead calm, then slight southwest, then west, then northwest, all in a span of 20 minutes. Then all hell broke loose as it quickly came up to hurricane force, northwesterly. What was sporadic hunting turned into unbelievable action, you couldn't hardly keep shells in your gun, it was reload, reload, reload. But when we left the shelter of the rush bed to retrieve birds, the blind we had around the boat acted as a sail and the boat started to go over, the wind was so fierce. Had it gone over, that would have been the end of us in that wind and cold water, tangled in the chicken wire blind. But we quickly threw it overboard just in the nick of time, the boat righted, we retrieved the blind before it sank and the ducks and got the heck out of there.

CHAPTER 4

Another time I had two others in the boat on a late-season hunt, one of them quite an old man who was somewhat frail. When the wind achieved hurricane levels (only a slight exaggeration) we fled, having to quarter into the wind to keep the waves from coming over the bow. Although I went at only half-throttle, the spray so coated us that we were fully glazed with ice by the time we reached the shore. This poor old guy needed help just to get back into the truck, he was so coated with ice.

The third time it happened, the hurricane came from the south. The next day I had to go get the decoys and I knew it would require me to go past the "motorboat limit" to get them all. God alone knew how far they had been blown, so I called the game warden and left a message on his answering machine, telling him exactly what had happened and what I was about to do. I did the deed and I never heard back from him. Either I finished the task before he got the message or he possessed a good amount of common sense, meaning the violation was petty compared to my getting my decoys back, something that had to be done and brought harm to no one. I'll never know and I sure wasn't going to ask later.

We've been checked by quite a few game wardens over the years, it's always been pleasant and they have treated us with dignity and respect. Jim Loftness was the greatest warden we have ever met out there, he was so respectful of the public and yet you knew that if you got stupid, he would pop you in a New York minute. So we didn't get stupid. One fall I was filming those beautiful golden basswoods along the Johnson road by the sandpit on the west end and along comes Jim. He stopped and we exchanged pleasantries. It was one of those rare, fall days where everything was perfect – the sky was a brilliant blue, there was a mild but chilly northwest breeze, the leaves were bathed in golden drops of sunlight and you wished you didn't have to ever leave that spot, ever. Then Jim told me that this was about the end for him and that he was going to be done soon, his career was about over. There was a little heaviness in his voice and I could feel it coming out of him. For a moment there were only two people in the whole wide world, just Jim and me – and we were on the same level, it was man to man, not warden to hunter. And then he was done, and eventually we got a new, young warden with nowhere near the social skills as Jim. We still miss him.

Without doubt, the greatest hunt we never had was when my son Tom was in high school. I had been pulling him out of school every fall when the weather said "go hunting," and it had worked all those years because he kept his grades up despite his many absences. (Eventually the principal called and set a limit, we didn't exactly see eye to eye but somehow it all worked out in the end). We had been having trouble with the nut and bolt that holds the oarlock to the oar, and I had told my young Tom that he needed to tighten that bolt, a simple task. But he never did. Then the mother of all duck mornings came, and we said to each other "let's go," and off we went. The wind was off the charts but we knew a safe way to get out there, and once there we would be protected by the rush beds. So off we went, into the dark cauldron of a wind-swept Lake Christina. Unfortunately, the motor wouldn't start despite all of the tricks I had in my bag. That left us the oars, and with the hope of a great hunt within us, we each grabbed one and started a "double row." Within a minute the strain against that wind popped that loose oarlock, the nut and bolt were lost and we were done for. What was said at that moment shall go unrepeated. Not yet ready to give up, we still had the 12' push-pole, but against that wind we just couldn't control the 14' boat. At last we were finished. We sat there in the darkness, pounded against the shore by the waves and hopelessly defeated, knowing there was a duck hunt in an hour that we would be missing. We got out of the boat into knee-deep water and pushed it along shore back to the access, a dejected pair. Tom got off to school on time and I went to work, but that howling wind wouldn't leave me alone, so around 9 am I drove back down to the lake to see what she looked like. I will never forget what I saw. I have never, not before or since, seen waterfowl like I saw on that day. The sky was filled with endless groups of ducks working the lake. There was no end to the ducks, they were on the water and in the air and everywhere between. It was a migration morning and we weren't out there, we had missed the greatest duck hunt that we could have ever had. It still hurts to this day.

In the early years we never used duck calls, but then I hunted with wildlife photographer Dale Spartas and he worked magic on Mallards like I've never seen. Instantly I became a believer. He gave me his call at the end of that hunt, but there was much to learn. So we learned to call ducks (both dippers and divers) out there in the early morning darkness. The birds roost in the rush beds in the evenings and maybe an hour or two before first light they begin to talk to each other as they awake. That's a golden opportunity to listen to and learn from wild birds instead of some cassette tape. We'd get our calls out and try to match the live birds, and at first we sounded disastrous. Then we'd tear our calls apart and adjust the reeds, either in or out, and eventually we would capture the right tones. But there was still volume and cadence to learn and master, and that took many, many "sessions" in the early morning darkness. Eventually we nailed it down pretty good and whether it be divers or dippers, we learned from our failures as well as our successes. We now call heavily, to the point that other hunters around the lake give us a ration about the "endless calling" coming from the House boat. We will quit when it quits working for us, and that's all I'm going to say.

As to frequency of hunting, I have been fortunate enough (or unlucky, you make the call) to be self-employed and somewhat have the luxury of hunting when I wish to, living close to the lake. A constant problem with that has been Beaver Johnson who owns the sandpit on the west end. I once asked him how he got his name and he told me that when he was young, he was "busy as a beaver" and the name stuck. He's still that way today, and very often while hunting we can hear him in the far distance, working on his dozer or his loader or with his dump trucks. Then the guilt hits us that we should be working too and that can have a dampening effect on the whole hunt. So one year a bunch of us talked about it and we were going to draft a petition and all sign it and present it to Beaver, appealing to his humanity and requesting that for mercy's sake, could he please just lay off until noon? The guilt was killing us. We never did it, but we should have.

One morning the wind was particularly wild, out of the northwest. We were the first ones on the rough lake, and got a sheltered spot where the wind wouldn't beat us up. A little while later we heard another boat go out from the access, farther out into the lake than we were. Ten minutes later, in the pitch black and the roaring wind, we heard cries for help and three gunshots. In an instant we knew that they were in trouble, every boat hunter fears this exact situation and finally here it was on our doorstep. We couldn't just leave them out there in that maelstrom, so we headed farther out in our two boats, one 12' and one 14', already loaded with hunters and gear, in an attempt to save these poor bastards. Long story short, we got these three guys into our two little boats in waves that would curl your hair, and got them into shore. They were from southern Minnesota and they had plowed out into that nightmare in a jonboat – a JONBOAT! They were doomed before they even started the motor. But later that day, after they had dried out and warmed up, we helped them back out there and got as much of their gear as could be found. All's well that ends well, I guess. We haven't seen them since.

I have gone out there in fog so heavy that I got lost on the way and had to stop due to motion sickness, just shy of puking over the side. We have gone out with almost no sleep and with more than one hangover. I have sat in our dining room in Melby and out of the corner of my eye, have seen migrating ducks over head. Upon running outside there were tens of thousands of canvasbacks low overhead, having just left the lake, heading southeast towards Chesapeake Bay. We've seen 25,000 canvasbacks leave the lake in 10 minutes one evening around the end of October. At those times you watch in awe and wonder and wish you could fly with them. My son Tom shot his first duck on the wing on that lake, a big bull Redhead. What a celebration that was for a 10 year old! Contrast that with the time Tom dropped his Remington 870 into the drink, in about four and a half feet of water. I asked him what he weighed and it turned out that I was the heavier of us two. I told him that I was staying in the boat and that he was going swimming, and over the side he went, holding his breath while I held his belt from behind. The first time down he found nothing; the second time he came up with his $350 gun. We continued to hunt.

I've had mornings on Lake Christina where we never fired a shot, and I've had a flock of 400 Bluebills decoy in belly-up. My gun had jammed 20 minutes earlier and the other guy was so spellbound by the sight that he began shooting only after I hollered at him to shoot. I have been a quarter mile from shore with the same guy and had an ice floe rip my 12' homemade wooden boat apart and come that close to sending us to a watery grave, but for the grace of God and hard bailing. I've shot Black Ducks and oldsquaws on that lake, presumably off course. I remember hearing Virgil Palmquist, whose Swedish grandfather had homesteaded on the south side of the lake, tell me that at times when hunting the lake in the "good old days," he would hear thunder when the sky was clear and blue, and upon looking towards the sound, would see 10,000 canvasbacks that had gotten up to stretch and fly around.

Lake Christina is where I taught my two sons to endure hardship and to get out of bed at an early hour and how to shoot moving targets at 50 miles per hour in a bobbing boat, how to be patient when the birds are still coming towards the decoys and how to forgive themselves when they're in a shooting slump and can't hit anything. Hunting the rushes is where you can, no, you must talk without pretense, because phoniness just doesn't fit out there. It's where you are simultaneously as relaxed as you will ever be, and as tense as you can be when a flock has taken a shine to your spread of decoys and has crossed that invisible line from out-of-range to safeties off. There are times when it's hard to breathe, you're so wound up. Out there is where cigars and coffee are at their absolute finest and where the air couldn't possibly be fresher.

I've seen migration mornings where your jaw is left hanging from the sights and sounds of flock after flock of new birds. We've made honest mistakes and had accidents happen that give you great pause; but this is life and we continue to go, knowing the risks. There is no telling what the day will bring, that's part of the mystique and drama and adventure that is boat hunting the rushes. I have seen the lake strong and healthy and I have seen it deader than a doornail. Healthy is better. We are all in high hopes of a permanent solution so that "this old girl" is saved forever. Every year it's getting more challenging for my sore knees, boat hunting large public water is a very tough sport between the early hours and the cold and the dark and

CHAPTER 4

outboard motors and the competition and setting out and then picking up decoys. It's for men younger than me. But as long as I can cram my body in and out of a duck boat at four in the morning, I guess I'll be out there.

Hand carved Canvasback decoys by John House

LAKE CHRISTINA COOKBOOK

Lake Christina with markings denoting the camps locations and other historic locations, Courtesy of Mark Reineke and JOR Engineering.

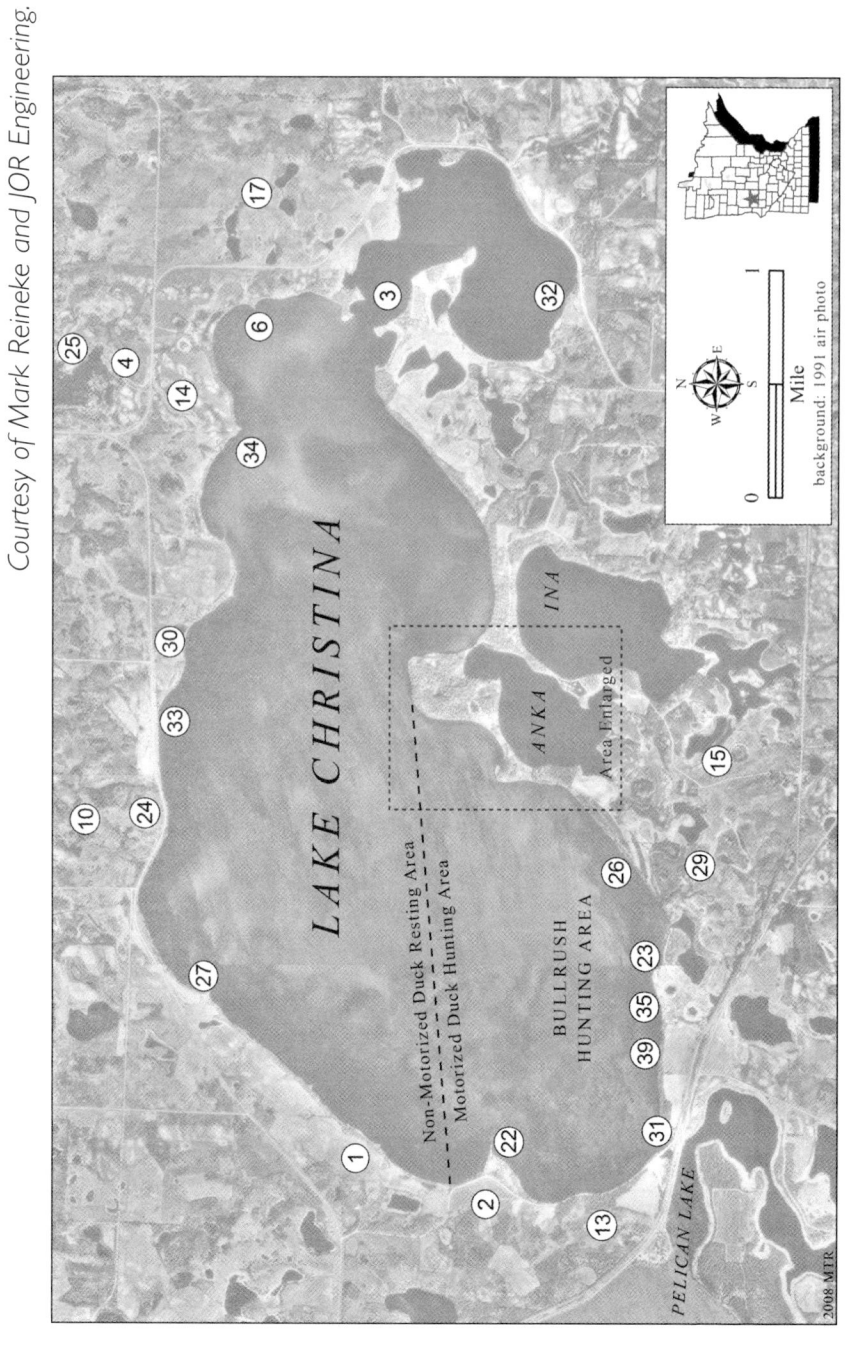

82

CHAPTER 4

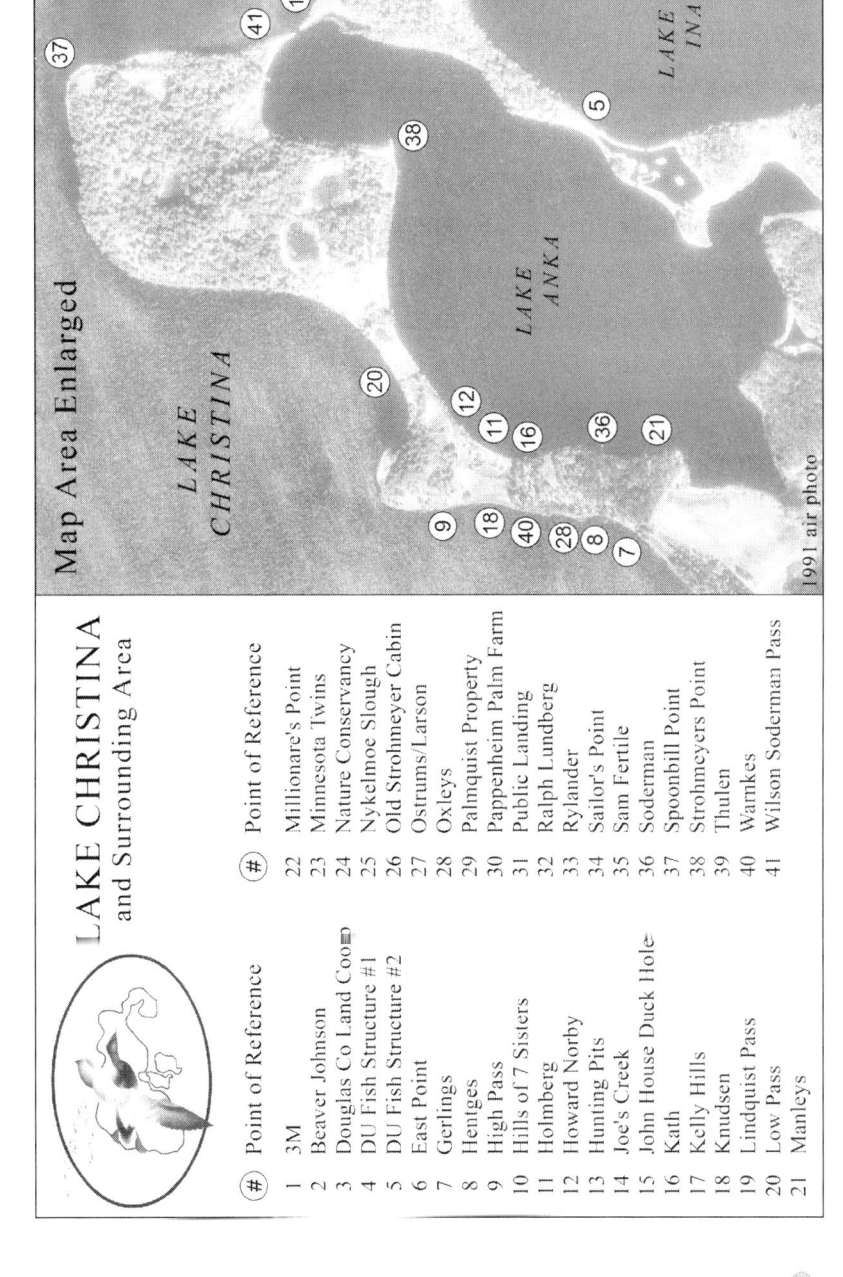

LAKE CHRISTINA
and Surrounding Area

Map Area Enlarged

LAKE CHRISTINA · *LAKE ANKA* · *LAKE INA*

1991 air photo

#	Point of Reference	#	Point of Reference
1	3M	22	Millionare's Point
2	Beaver Johnson	23	Minnesota Twins
3	Douglas Co Land Coop	24	Nature Conservancy
4	DU Fish Structure #1	25	Nykelmoe Slough
5	DU Fish Structure #2	26	Old Strohmeyer Cabin
6	East Point	27	Ostrums/Larson
7	Gerlings	28	Oxleys
8	Hentges	29	Palmquist Property
9	High Pass	30	Pappenheim Palm Farm
10	Hills of 7 Sisters	31	Public Landing
11	Holmberg	32	Ralph Lundberg
12	Howard Norby	33	Rylander
13	Hunting Pits	34	Sailor's Point
14	Joe's Creek	35	Sam Fertile
15	John House Duck Hole	36	Soderman
16	Kath	37	Spoonbill Point
17	Kelly Hills	38	Strohmeyers Point
18	Knudsen	39	Thulen
19	Lindquist Pass	40	Warnkes
20	Low Pass	41	Wilson Soderman Pass
21	Manleys		

83

Lake Christina Cookbook

Chapter 5
Duck & Goose Recipes

*Left, early paper Carrylite goose decoy
Right, Oscar Quam goose decoy*

Slow Cooker Goose Breasts

By Paulette Dalum

4-6 goose breasts
Enough chicken or beef broth to cover
1 can cream of celery soup
1 can cream of mushroom soup
1 sliced onion
salt and pepper, garlic optional

Cook all day on low.

Strain juice off and add cream of celery and cream of mushroom soups. Use the juice to make gravy. Cover breasts in gravy and serve!

Candied Duck

By Banquet Attendee 07

1 or 2 large duck breasts,
    cut into strips 1/2" wide by 2-1/2" long
2 large apples
2 cups flour
4 servings prepared white rice
1/2 cup unsalted butter
1 cup brown sugar
1 tsp salt
1 tsp pepper

Peel and slice the apples, place them on a flat surface (cookie sheet). Sprinkle brown sugar over the apples and let set for 1 hour or until the brown sugar becomes syrupy. Dust the meat strips in seasoned flour, place in fry pan or skillet and cook over medium heat in unsalted butter until almost done. Pour the apples/sugar mixture into the fry pan, cover and simmer 15-20 minutes until apples are tender and slightly crisp.

Goose Enchiladas
By Banquet/ Fundraiser Attendee 06

5-6 goose breasts
1 package taco seasoning
2 cans enchilada sauce
12 tortilla shells (pre-made or purchased)
3 cups shredded cheese
2 cups chopped onion

Grind the goose breasts into burger, brown in skillet, add package of taco seasoning, 2 cans enchilada sauce, mix well over medium heat.

Fill taco shells with goose meat, onions and cheese, Place in cake pan and heat at 350° for 15 minutes or until shells are golden brown.

Goose or Duck Wild Rice
By Paulette Dalum

goose or duck, cut up
3 cups chicken broth
1-1/2 cups wild rice
1/2 cup sunflower seeds
2 bay leaves
1 can cream of celery soup
pepper to taste (no salt)
1 tsp Worcestershire

Bake at 325° for two hours.

DUCK & GOOSE RECIPES

Duck with Jack Daniels
By Paul & Gerry Thompson & Ducks Unlimited

6-8 duck breasts (skin intact)
Kosher salt and fresh black pepper
1 Tbsp olive oil
1 Tbsp butter
1/2 cup beef broth
1/4 cup Jack Daniels
1-1/2 cups thin sliced mushrooms
1/3 cup heavy whipping cream
cloves garlic
1/4 cup diced red onion
1 Tbsp brown sugar

Liberally season duck breasts with salt and pepper. Heat oil and butter in a large cast iron skillet over medium-high heat. Add breasts, skin side down and cook until medium brown, about 4 minutes. Flip breasts and cook for 3 minutes. Remove breasts and allow to rest. Add garlic, onion, brown sugar and stir and cook 3-4 minutes. Stir in beef broth and reduce liquid by 50%. Add Jack Daniels, cook 2 minutes. Add mushrooms and sauté until tender. Add cream and cook until slightly thickened. Return duck breasts to pan and cook until med-rare. Remove breasts and slice diagonally into 1/4" slices. Pour mushrooms and sauce over duck breasts.

Goose Breast / Coot Recipe
By Glenn Gausman (long time member of the Oxley Camp)

Skinned boneless fillet of goose breast or coot breasts, cut in chunks.

Roll chunks in flour, garlic powder, seasoned salt, and pan brown.

Place chunks in cake pan with 1/2" water, some mild onion slices, small handful of "allspice" and bake at 250° for 30 minutes. Turn over meat and bake for another 30 minutes. Serve over wild rice, noodles or whatever!

Goose or Duck on Grill

By Ranae Edwards

1 goose or duck breast cut into 1-1/2" chunks
1/2 cup soy sauce
1/2 cup olive oil
minced garlic (to taste)

Prep time: 20 minutes, actual cooking time 10 minutes

Cut pieces of meat into 1-1/2" chunks. Marinate 4 hours or overnight in the soy sauce, olive oil and garlic, turning every couple of hours to coat. Wrap each piece of marinated meat in 1/2 slice of bacon (which has been pre-cooked for 1 minute in microwave. Secure bacon to meat with a wooden toothpick. Grill at medium-low setting on top rack of grill for about 4-5 minutes on each side, turning only once. Do not over cook and do not burn bacon. Best tasting if served med to med-rare.

Jelly Braised Duck Breast

By Jon Schneider, MN Ducks Unlimited Biologist

4-6 duck breasts
Raspberry vinaigrette salad dressing

Glaze

1/2 jar blackberry current jelly
1/2 cup red wine

Mix jelly and wine in saucepan, heat and stir.

Place plucked duck, breasts side down in roasting pan, drizzle 1/2 bottle of raspberry vinaigrette salad dressing in and over ducks. Slow roast at 225° for 4-8 hours. To serve, carefully remove the ducks and de-bone. Serve meat warm with fruit-based glaze finish.

DUCK & GOOSE RECIPES

Goose Droppings Hors D'oeuvres
By Jim & Kandace Norby
(family hunting tradition on Christina & Anka extends 4 generations)

1 goose breast	Italian salad dressing
flour	oil for frying
favorite seasoning salt	

Slice goose breast 1/2" thick and marinate in salad dressing in a bowl for 4 hours. Drain and coat with flour. Fry in hot oil in skillet for 4 minutes per side. Season with salt and cut into goose-sized droppings and serve.

Duck or Goose Stew
By Ranae Edwards/ Chef John

4 cups duck or goose meat cut in 1" cubes	
1/4 cup vegetable oil	2 bay leaves
1/2 cup flour	1 tsp salt
1 cup onions, cut in 1/2" cubes	1 tsp black pepper
1 cup celery, cut in 1/2" cubes	3 cups beef stock
2 cups carrots, cut in 1/4" slices	3 cups diced tomatoes, with juice
1 cup turnips or parsnips, cut in 1/4" slices	1 tsp dried thyme
2 cloves garlic, diced fine	1/2 cup dill pickle juice
3 cups potatoes, peeled and cut in 1" cubes	

In a large skillet heat oil to smoke hot. Roll meat in flour and shake off excess. Add meat to oil and brown. Remove meat.

Add onion, celery, carrots, turnips, garlic and sauté for 5 minutes. Add bay leaves, salt, pepper, and remaining flour and stir gently. Remove ingredients to a Dutch oven, add meat cubes and remaining ingredients, except for potatoes. Cover and bake at 350° for 1-1/2 hours. Add potatoes and stir gently from bottom. Bake 30 minutes or until potatoes are tender.

Wild Duck and Wild Rice

By Dan Johnson

1 cup Uncle Ben's wild rice
3-4 tsp sage
4-5 stalks diced celery
1 can cream of mushroom soup
1 cup cashews, chopped
4 cups water
1/2 cup butter
1 medium onion
3/4 cup soy sauce

Salt and pepper bird. Roast in roaster pan at 400° for 1 hour. Baste with butter and soy sauce.

Prepare wild rice. Mix rice, water and sage, bring to a boil cover and simmer about 30 minutes then fluff with a fork

Sauté butter, celery, onion. Take meat off bones, add meat and stock from roaster pan, add cream of mushroom soup and soy sauce. Add cashews on top. Cover and bake 20 minutes.

Pan-Fried Duck Breast & Sherry Sauce

By Country Kitchen & Teresa Marrone

2 duck breasts, skinned
lemon pepper
2 Tbsp butter
2 Tbsp raspberry jam
celery salt
1 small onion
3/4 cup sherry

Sprinkle duck breasts on both sides with celery salt and lemon pepper and set aside. Peel onion, chop and set aside. In a heavy medium skillet, melt butter over med heat and add duck breasts. Cook about 3 minutes then turn, and add onion. Cook another 3 minutes While the second side cooks, blend the sherry and jam. Pour the mixture over the duck breast and continue to cook for another 4-7 minutes until just pink inside. Slice breasts across grain to serve.

DUCK & GOOSE RECIPES

Duck Fillets
By Lyman Game & Fish Cookery

1/2 cup flour
1/2 tsp paprika
1/2 stick butter
1/2 pint sour cream
dash soy sauce
salt and pepper, to taste
8-12 duck breast fillets
1 can cream of mushroom
dash Worcestershire

Combine flour, salt pepper, and paprika in a bag. Add duck breast fillets and shake to coat. Sauté in butter over low heat until tender. Add soup, soy sauce and Worcestershire. Cook until bubbly. Place fillets in 9x13" baking dish, spoon sour cream over top and bake at 325° for 30 minutes.

Goose Wraps
By Banquet / Fundraiser Attendee 05

goose breasts
zesty Italian salad dressing
green peppers, sliced
onion slices
honey

Marinate chopped 1" goose breasts in zesty Italian dressing for 1-2 days.

Wrap goose chunks with green peppers, onion slices and bacon. Cook on grill low heat until medium rare. Add honey over pieces last minute or two on grill.

Wild Goose Crock Pot
By Scott DeMesy

1 can cream of mushroom soup
1 can cream of onion soup
1 can water
1 cup chopped onions
1 cup chopped carrots

Separate wings, legs, thighs and place breast (meat down) in crock pot. Add all ingredients. Pepper, salt, to taste. Cook covered on low heat for 8-10 hours.

Dark Cherry Ducks
By Dave "Dancin" Manley
(this family has hunted Christina and fished Anka since the 1940s)

1 large or 2 small ducks
1 can 16oz. pitted dark cherries
1 Tbsp butter
1 Tbsp vegetable oil
1 small onion, chopped
1 Tbsp flour
1/2 cup water
2 Tbsp cream sherry
1 tsp brown sugar
1 tsp instant bouillon granules
1/2 tsp ground cinnamon
1/4 tsp salt
1-2 Tbsp cornstarch
1-2 Tbsp water

Drain cherries, reserving 1/2 cup of juice. Set aside. In Dutch oven melt butter and oil over medium heat. Add onion and cook till tender, Add duck pieces and brown on all sides, remove and set aside. Stir flour into onion mixture. Stir in reserved cherry juice, water, sherry, brown sugar, bouillon, cinnamon and salt. Add duck and cherries, heat to boiling. Reduce heat and cover. Simmer until tender, 1-1/2 to 2 hours (turning pieces once). Transfer ducks to platter, set aside and keep warm. Skim sauce. If thinner than desired, blend 2 Tbsp of corn starch in 2 Tbsp of water and cook over medium heat until thickened. Serve over duck pieces.

Wild Duck Wild Rice Soup
By Banquet/ Fundraiser Attendee 06

1 cup wild rice
1/2 cup diced carrots
1/2 cup diced celery
3/4 lb bacon, fried and diced
2 cans unsweetened condensed milk
1 small can water chestnuts
salt and pepper, to taste
1 lb wild duck (pellets removed)
1 can cream of potato soup
1 can cream of mushroom soup
2-3 Tbsp of butter

Dice duck and fry with butter. Set aside. In a large soup pot add cooked wild rice, carrots, celery, cooked bacon, condensed milk, water chestnuts, cream of potato, cream of mushroom and salt and pepper. Bring to a slight boil while stirring. Simmer for 30-45 minutes. If soup is too thick, add milk or water.

Wild Duck Cheese Puffs
By Tyler Wirth

1/2 lb duck
1 cup shredded cheese
1 tube Pillsbury crescents
3-4 Tbsp mayonnaise

Preheat oven to 375°. Cook duck in oven, remove and dice. Mix diced duck meat, shredded cheese and mayonnaise in large bowl. Open and unroll Pillsbury crescents. Do not pull apart triangles (2 triangles equals a square dough piece). Separate crescents into squares. Spoon the duck cheese mixture into middle of dough. Bring corners of square together and pinch until all sides are sealed. Cook in oven per directions on tube. Note: may take longer due to filling.

Jalapeño Duck

By Jason Law

As many boneless, skinless duck breasts as required, (ring neck, wood duck, small mallards)

Create a "pita-pocket" lengthwise in duck breast. Invert duck breast to improve marinating, Marinade in sealed container overnight or longer.

Jason's preferred marinade
1/3 vegetable oil, 1/3 soy sauce 1/3 Lawry's mesquite marinade.

Remove duck breasts and discard marinade. Place a piece of cheese (Swiss, Monterey Jack, or Pepper Jack) into cavity. Place 1-3 jalapeño slices (fresh or from jar) into cavity. Wrap breasts with bacon and hold with toothpicks. Grill breasts indirect method or on top shelf for 20 minutes, rotating every 5 minutes. Warning: Be careful as too many jalapeños may make for extra beer consumption

Baked Christina Duck

By Johnny Lindquist
(if you are one of the lucky neighbors or hunting companions, you have had this duck recipe)

4 large picked ducks
1 turkey-size oven bag
seasoned salt or coarse ground salt
celery, onion, apple, orange

Rub inside of cavity with salt. Stuff cavity with quartered fruits and vegetables. Rub skin with salt. Place in oven bag and Bake at 300° for 2 to 2-1/2 hours. Turn heat up to 325° until breast bone protrudes. Serves 4-6 hunters.

Southwestern Grilled Duck with Chipotle-Apricot Glaze

By Ducks Unlimited

6 duck or small goose breasts

Brine	**Glaze**
1 gallon water	1 - 12 oz jar apricot jam
1/2 cup honey	1-2 Tbsp chipotle peppers in adobe sauce, very finely diced
1/4 cup dark brown sugar	
5 Tbsp salt	
3 Tbsp cilantro, minced	
1 Tbsp pickling spice	
2 tsp garlic powder	
1 tsp onion powder	

Prepare brine and stir. Add breasts, store in fridge for minimum 6 hours, preferably overnight.

To prepare chipotle-apricot glaze, add jam and diced peppers to a saucepan and bring to simmer for 5 minutes.

Remove duck/goose fillets from brine and pat dry. Cook fillets over hot grill, 3 minutes per side.

Allow fillets to rest for 3-5 minutes prior to slicing. Slice fillets at an angle and generously pour glaze over fillets.

This recipe was awarded 1st place in Ducks Unlimited 2007 contest – you'll see why!!

ENJOY!

Duck Creole
By Ducks Unlimited

2 cups boneless duck breast cut into 1" strips
2 Tbsp vegetable oil
2 Tbsp butter
1 cup diced yellow onions
3/4 cup diced green bell pepper
4 garlic cloves, minced
2 bay leaves
1 tsp dried basil leaves
2/3 cup canned tomato sauce
4 cups warm cooked rice
3 Tbsp Cajun spice
1 cup diced celery
1/2 tsp Tabasco sauce
2 cups chicken stock
1 tsp dried thyme leaves
1-1/2 cups peeled diced tomato
1 tsp sugar

Heat oil in large skillet over medium-high heat. Season duck pieces with Cajun spice and add to skillet. Sear duck evenly until well browned. Remove duck from skillet, add butter, onion, celery and bell pepper, sauté for 5 minutes or until softened. Return duck to skillet and add Tabasco, garlic, chicken broth, bay leaves, thyme and basil. Simmer for 1 hour, covered. Add tomato, tomato sauce and sugar. Simmer until duck is tender and sauce has thickened to your liking. Adjust seasonings and serve over warm rice.

Duck Roll Appetizer
By Brian Ingals

8 wild duck breasts, fileted to 1/2" thick slices
1 onion, cut in wedges
Italian salad dressing
Bacon

Marinade duck slices in salad dressing overnight. Remove and pat dry. Wrap duck slices around a onion wedge and wrap it in 1/2 bacon strip. Attach with toothpick. Grill on med-low until bacon is done.

DUCK & GOOSE RECIPES

Lindquist's Canada Goose & Sauce
By Johnny Lindquist
(this sauce is very good, I didn't think he'd part with it)

1 picked Canada goose	Lawry's season salt
onion, apple, celery	1 can pears
1 can cranberries	1 sm jar diced candied apple rings
4 cans Mandarin oranges	2 cups honey
3 cups applesauce	1 turkey size oven bag

Rub goose skin and cavity with Lawry's season salt. Quarter fruits and vegetables and fill in cavity. Place in oven bag and bake at 300° for 2-1/2 hours. Turn up heat to 325° until breast bone is protruding under skin. Remove meat from carcass and place on platter with an individual serving bowl of sauce.

Sauce:
Put pears, cranberries, candied apple rings, and Mandarin oranges in blender and blend until smooth. Place in mixing bowl and add honey and applesauce. Cook for 1 hour over medium heat. Can be frozen and used again.

Annandale Buttered Wild Duck & Rice
By Karen & Hazel Gruss
(Gramma Hazel made sure my father loved the outdoors and hunting)

3 diver ducks	1 gallon of water
1/2 tsp garlic powder	1/2 tsp onion powder
1/2 tsp black pepper	1/2 tsp season salt

Drop cleaned, plucked ducks in simmering water containing all the spices. Cook until the duck is tender. Throw out liquid, and cut ducks in half. Brown duck halves in butter in cast iron skillet. Remove ducks and stuff cavities with favorite wild rice recipe. Serve with orange glaze on side. (see side dishes)

Christina Duck & Goose Marinade
By Gwen Lillemon (Daughter of Joe Gradin)

2 lbs duck or goose breasts, cubed
1 cup buttermilk   1- 16 oz Italian salad dressing
thin sliced bacon

Place buttermilk and dressing in a plastic bowl and cover. Refrigerate for 5 days stirring daily. Remove meat wrap with bacon fasten with toothpick and grill for 10 -15 minutes.

Duck Egg Rolls
By Ducks Unlimited

1-1/2 cups boneless/skinless duck breasts
2 Tbsp soy sauce   1 tsp minced fresh ginger
2 garlic cloves, minced   2 Tbsp peanut oil
1/4 cup dried apricots thinly sliced 1-1/2 c green cabbage shredded
8 egg roll wrappers
1 Tbsp corn starch mixed with 1 Tbsp cold water
oil for frying

Dipping Sauce
1/4 cup soy sauce   1 Tbsp Hoison sauce
2 Tbsp rice vinegar or white vinegar   1 Tbsp brown sugar

Combine sliced duck with soy sauce, ginger, garlic and marinate for 30 minutes. Drain ducks. Stir-fry duck in hot peanut oil for 45-60 seconds over high heat in a wok or skillet. Transfer to paper towels and cool. For each duck roll, lay the wrapper on a flat surface. Place about 2-3 tablespoons of the cabbage on the lower third of the wrapper forming an area about 1" tall by 3" wide. Arrange apricots and cooked duck on top of cabbage. Turn in the sides of the wrapper to just overlap stuffing. Begin rolling, starting at the edge, moisten it with a little of the cornstarch mixture to help it seal. Place roll in hot oil, enough to submerse it and fry until golden brown. Drain on paper towels. Combine sauce ingredients and serve with duck rolls.

Duck Gumbo

By James L Davis

1 large or 2 small ducks
1 tsp peanut oil
3/4 cup bacon crumbs
1 cup onions diced
4 Tbsp flour
1 tsp seasoned salt
1 cup green onions
1 cup parsley, chopped
3 tsp chili powder
1 tsp mustard powder
1 tsp white pepper
1/2 tsp pepper relish
1 lb smoked link sausage
1 can shrimp and or oysters
1 can tomato
1/4 tsp red pepper

Cook bacon crumbs, onion and flour to a desired color. Add water and seasonings. Add duck and boil 1 hour. (Leave whole or debone into bite size pieces) Cut sausage in small pieces and add. Add tomato, shrimp and/or oysters. Cook another 1-1/2 hours and serve over rice.

Duck Gumbo

By Larry Crain

2-3 duck breasts, cubed
1 clove garlic
1 cup bell pepper
1 tsp red pepper
1 lb spicy sausage
1 cup onion
1 cup celery
1/4 tsp thyme
Tony Checkers Creole seasoning (to taste)

Flour duck breast cubes and brown, remove and set aside. Fry sausage and set aside. Sauté remaining vegetables and seasonings – do not over cook!

Roux
In a large skillet, mix 1 cup oil and 1 cup flour, stir constantly over low heat until the mixture is the color of cream in coffee.

Add sautéed vegetables, duck and sausage. Adjust thickness with chicken broth if necessary. Serve over rice.

Low Slow Roasted Canvasback with Kraut

By Jon Schneider, Minnesota DU Biologist

1-2 plucked canvasback
1 large jar sauerkraut, preferably fresh
1/2 cup brown sugar

Soak plucked duck in salt water overnight in refrigerator. Place duck in Dutch oven roaster or very large slow cooker. Mix entire jar of sauerkraut and brown sugar together and fill duck cavities. Place remainder of kraut over birds. Cover and cook slowly at a temperature of 200-250° for 4-6 hours. Remove meat and separate all skin and fat prior to serving with remaining kraut. Recommend green beans with almonds and fresh warm bread or rolls. Enjoy with a red Cabernet.

Canada Goose In Rice & Veggie Hotdish

By Banquet Attendee 05

1 Canada goose breast
1/2 medium onion
3 bay leaves
Beef Rice A Roni
12 baby carrots
2-3 stalks of celery
water to cover
butter

Chop celery and onion. Place goose breast and all ingredients in a crock pot on low for 8-10 hours.

Remove the breast, save the liquid and throw away the vegetables. Slice the breast into bite size pieces.

Chop up new vegetables; carrots, celery, onion.

Prepare the Rice A Roni per box directions, substituting the water with the saved goose liquid.

Combine the goose pieces, vegetables, and rice in a casserole dish and bake at 350° for 1 hour or until tender.

Brad's Mild Indian Duck
By Brad Gruss

10-15 duck breasts
Lawry's season salt
onion powder
buttered flavored popcorn oil

lemon pepper
garlic powder

Preheat cast iron skillet with butter flavored popcorn oil, approximately 1/2" in depth.

Make cross grain incisions in each duck breast approximately 3/8" apart. Cut approximately 1/2 to 3/4 the way through the breast. Carefully hand wash duck breast under cold running water, kneading and rinsing until the majority of blood is rinsed from the breast. With experience you can control the flavor (game taste) from none to full flavor by rinsing time and amount of seasoning.

Pat dry with paper towels and season with above seasonings. Allow to stand for 15 minutes or longer.

Place duck in skillet, cook fast and hot, approximately 30 seconds per side. Remove when med-rare. Enjoy!

Duck Confit
By Chef Charlie Gruss

2 lbs duck legs/thighs
1 tsp black peppercorns
1 bay leaf
1 Tbsp brown sugar
1 lb duck fat (rendered)

1 oz Kosher salt
4 each Juniper berries
1 Tbsp garlic (minced)
4 sprigs fresh thyme (minced)

Combine spices and grind coarsely in a clean coffee grinder. Mix spices, salt, sugar, garlic, and thyme together and rub on duck legs and thighs. Cure overnight. Rinse rub off the next day, pat dry and let dry uncovered in refrigerator overnight. In a large pot, bring duck fat to a low simmer and cook duck until braised, approximately 2-3 hours. Any unused meat can be kept cool covered in the duck fat (used as a preservative).

Duck Breast Rumaki

By Glen Bean　　　　　　　　　　Makes 16 to 20 appetizers

2 boneless breast halves, med to large wild ducks
1/2 cup sake or dry sherry　　8-10 bacon slices, halved
1 Tbsp soy sauce　　　　　　　16-20 canned whole
1 Tbsp peanut oil　　　　　　　　　　water chestnuts
1 tsp minced fresh ginger root

Cut each breast half into 8 to 10 pieces, about 1" wide. In small mixing bowl, blend sake, soy sauce, oil and ginger root. Add duck pieces; stir to coat. Marinate at room temperature for 1 hour, or in refrigerator overnight.

Place 1 duck piece and 1 water chestnut on a piece of bacon. Wrap bacon around water chestnut/duck piece. Secure with toothpick. Repeat until all duck pieces are used.

Heat oven to broil (550°). Arrange appetizers on broiler pan. Broil 3 to 4 inches from heat coil until bacon is at desired doneness, about 7-10 minutes. Turn once. (Alternate cooking method is to do on grill, to desired doneness.)

Note: Be sure to have enough on-hand. These are quite addictive, and even the most skeptical game eater, will likely devour them!!!

Goose a la Crème

By Glen Bean　　　　　　　　　　　　　　　　Serves 4

Skin goose, remove legs and breast. Cut breast into 1" thick pieces, cross-grain. Soak overnight in cool salt water. Pat dry.

Season with salt, pepper and sage - as desired. Roll in flour. Heat butter or cooking oil in skillet to frying temperature. Brown legs and breasts well on all sides. Place in glass covered casserole dish. Bake 1 hour at 325°.

Mix 2 cups half & half and two 10-1/2 ounce cans of mushroom soup. Pour over meat. Reduce heat to 275°, and bake until tender (about 2 hours).

Chapter 6
Big Game Recipes

Wrapped Venison Loin
By Earl J. Plattner, Sr.

3 lbs venison loin (whole)
1 lb thick sliced bacon
season salt
pepper

Roll venison loin in salt and pepper. Wrap bacon around loin to completely cover. Place in roasting pan and cover with aluminum foil. Bake at 250° (yes 250°) for 3 hours.

Note: Holland grill method – bring grill to temperature, grill 1/2 hour on each side.

Venison in Crock-Pot with Dressing
By Dave "Dancin" Manley

Slice venison steaks thin
6 slices of bacon, fried
1/4 tsp Lawry's season salt,
2 cups thin-chopped carrots
1 medium onion, chopped
1 cup Italian bread crumbs
parsley, celery salt, pepper to taste
2 cups chopped celery
3 cloves garlic, chopped

Season venison with season salt, parsley and pepper. Mix bread crumbs, garlic, celery, carrots and onions with a little water to make moist. Roll thin venison pieces around bread crumb mixture and connect with toothpick. Place in crock pot with butter and enough water to cover 1/2 of meat. Cook 3 hours.

Easiest Venison Ever
By Sue Soderman

2 lbs venison roast
McCormick's Montreal Steak Seasoning

Liberally shake steak seasoning on all sides of venison roast. Place in ziplock bag in refrigerator for 2 days. Cook on grill using indirect heat, approximately 1-1/2 hours at medium heat. Check after 1/2 hour to make sure heat isn't too high.

Venison Apple Chili
By Mark Skauge & Matt Muilen

5 lbs venison, cut in cubes	1/2 cup vegetable oil
5 onions diced	1/2 cup cumin
3 Tbsp chili powder	1 Tbsp pepper
5 Jalapeños, chopped fine	6 firm tart apples (peeled, diced)
1/2 cup garlic, chopped	2 cans tomato paste (6 oz)
3 cans crushed tomatoes (16 oz)	1 can tomato sauce (16 oz)
2 cups dry red wine	4 cups chicken stock
salt to taste	

Brown venison in oil. Add onions and sauté until tender. Pour off excess oil. Stir in spices, peppers, apples, and garlic, sauté for 10 minutes. Add everything else, bring to a boil, reduce heat and simmer for 2 hours. You can add beans, too, if you like (kidney, black or any other kind, 3-4 cans).

Venison Mushroom Simmer
By Micah Davids

2 lbs venison steak, (cut into thin strips)
2 Tbsp shortening
1 medium onion, chopped
1/4 cup soy sauce
2 beef bouillon cubes
Dash of pepper
1/4 cup cornstarch
1 med garlic, minced
1 4 oz can drained mushrooms
1 tsp salt
2-1/2 cups water

In a large skillet or wok, brown meat in shortening. Add onion and garlic cook until tender. Add soy sauce, mushrooms, bouillon, salt & pepper and 2 cups water. Cover and simmer. Combine cornstarch and 1/2 cup water and stir into mixture until thickened. Serve over rice or noodles.

Venison Burger Kraut Hotdish
By Sheila Johnson

1-1/2 lbs ground venison
1 15 oz can sauerkraut
1 can cream of celery soup
5 oz uncooked egg noodles
slices of American or Velveeta cheese
1 small chopped onion
1 can cream of mushroom soup
3/4 cup water

Brown venison and onion, place in 9x13" pan. Cover with sauerkraut. Heat soups and water, place dry noodles over sauerkraut, cover with soup mixture. Bake covered at 350° for 45 minutes. Top with cheese slices and return to oven until melted.

BIG GAME RECIPES

Venison on Weber Grill
By Brad Gruss

4-6 small venison steaks 1" to 1-1/2" thick
Garlic powder
Meat tenderizer
Wrights liquid smoke
3 cups red wine
Onion powder
Season salt
1 cup melted bacon grease
Black pepper

Take venison steaks out of freezer and place in plastic container. Add all seasonings (to taste) and mix with red wine. Allow venison to thaw in solution, 3-4 hours. Longer if in refrigerator.

Start Weber or charcoal grill, use direct method, wait until coals are very hot.

Melt bacon grease in microwave or stove top. Place steaks on grill directly over coals. Cook 1 minute, then liberally brush with melted bacon grease. When fire flares up, put grill cover on and cook 1 to 1-1/2 minutes. (depends on thickness of venison) Remove cover, turn meat and repeat process. Rare to medium rare with a seared surface.

Venison Buttermilk Roast
By Lyman Wild Gourmet

4 lb venison roast
vegetable oil for browning
salt and pepper
1 qt buttermilk
1/2 tsp garlic powder
1 onion sliced
frozen onion rings

Trim away all fat and brown roast in hot vegetable oil. Place in roaster and season with salt, pepper and garlic powder. Lay onions and onion rings on top and underneath roast. Pour 1 quart of buttermilk over roast and cook in 350° oven approximately 2-1/2 hours. Remove roast and slice. Reserve liquid from roast and make gravy.

Venison Pot Pie

By Harold Schmidt

1-1/2 lbs venison steak or roast, cut into 3/4" by 2" strips
3 Tbsp flour
2 med potatoes, skin on, chunked
1 cup beer
1 bay leaf
season salt (to taste)
garlic powder
1 ready made pie crust
1 cup bacon grease
2 medium onions
2 medium carrots, chopped
1/2 cup beef both
2 Tbsp tomato paste
cracked black pepper, to taste
1/4 tsp dried thyme
1/2 cup milk

Dust venison strips in flour and brown in bacon grease to rare. Remove and set on paper towels. Add onions, potatoes, bay leaf, carrots, all seasonings and sauté. Remove vegetables set aside, Add beer and de-glaze skillet. Add tomato paste, beef broth. Return all ingredients to skillet. Cook over medium for 15 minutes, or until mixture slightly thickens. Pour into baking dish, cover with premade pie crust and poke holes in crust. Bake at 450° 15-20 minutes or until pastry is cooked to your liking.

Bear Braised with Sweet Potatoes

By Lyman Wild Gourmet

4 lbs bear steak
3 stalks celery w/leaves, chopped
6 raw sweet potatoes
salt and pepper
2 cloves garlic minced
1 medium onion minced

Cut meat into 2" cubes, Brown in bacon drippings or vegetable oil. Put in roasting pan, add 1/2 cup water, garlic, onion and celery. Cover and bake at 350° (add water as needed to maintain moisture). Total cooking time is dependent on animal toughness. After 2 hours check for tenderness. When tender, add sweet potatoes sliced lengthwise and more water if necessary. Cover and cook until meat and potatoes are done.

BIG GAME RECIPES

Elk/Moose, Lamb & Beef Meatloaf
By Brad Gruss

1 lb of ground venison, elk or moose
with 1 lb of ground lamb and 1 lb of ground burger.

3 eggs	1 cup chopped onions
1 cup diced dill pickles	1 clove garlic minced
2 Tbsp soy sauce	2 Tbsp dark molasses
1/4 cup A1 sauce	2 cups crushed Ritz crackers
1/2 cup grated American cheese	1/2 cup grated pepper jack cheese
Cajun spice (to taste)	black pepper (to taste)
Italian seasoning (to taste)	2 cups ketchup

Beat eggs, add 3 lbs of ground meat, all seasonings andl other ingredients except ketchup. Knead and mix with hands in large bowl. Place in lightly greased baking dish and cover meat with 1/2" ketchup. Bake at 350° for 1 hour.

Sweet & Sour Venison Meatballs
By Jill Ingals
(We're still waiting for her corned beef venison roast recipe!)

1 lb venison burger	1/2 cup crushed corn flakes
1 egg	1/2 cup catsup
1 tsp chopped onion	

Sweet & Sour Sauce

3 oz grape jelly	6 oz chili sauce
1 heaping Tbsp brown sugar	1-1/2 tsp lemon juice

In a large pot, simmer grape jelly, chili sauce, brown sugar and lemon juice for 20 minutes.

Meanwhile, mix venison, corn flakes, egg, catsup and onion in a bowl and form 1" balls. Place on greased cookie sheet and bake 10-12 minutes at 350°. When done, place in sauce mixture and simmer 1/2 hour. Pour into deep serving dish and use toothpicks to serve hot!

Old Fashioned Game Pot Roast
By Chef John

2-3 lbs of boneless game meat cut into 2" cubes
1/4 cup olive oil   1/2 cup flour
2 cloves garlic, minced fine   2 cups onions, cubed 1"
1-1/2 cups parsnips or carrots cut into 1/4" slices
1/2 tsp nutmeg   1 tsp black pepper
1 Tbsp beef base   2 cups beef stock
1 cup dry sherry   2 cups fresh mushrooms
2 Tbsp tomato paste

Remove bones, fat and silver skin from game and cut into 2" cubes. Heat oil to almost smoke hot. Roll cubes in flour and shake off excess flour thoroughly. Add to oil and brown on all sides. Remove to a Dutch oven.

To the skillet add garlic, onions, parsnips/carrots and cook until tender. Add flour and gently combine. Add to meat. Add nutmeg, pepper, beef base, beef stock and sherry, Combine well. Cover and bake at 300° for 2 hours. Add mushrooms, tomato paste and gently combine. Return cover and bake for an additional 30 minutes.

Barbecue Venison Ribs
By Tom Welch

7-10 lbs venison ribs   12 oz Jack Daniels grilling sauce
4 oz Worcestershire   1 tsp liquid smoke

Cut ribs up into section of 3-4 ribs. Place in baking pan. Mix all ingredients and pour over ribs. Bake or grill until 3/4 done. Baste with sauce during cooking. Use leftover sauce to drizzle on ribs.

Bacon Wrapped Venison Tenderloin
By Mike Edwards

2-3 lbs venison tenderloin
4 oz steak sauce (Heinz 57, Bold A1)
1-2 lbs thin bacon slices
1 med onion, finely chopped
3 cloves garlic, finely chopped
brown sugar

Filet all white tendon tissue from outside of tenderloin (cut into strips as wide as bacon). Marinate in sauce of your choice, refrigerate for 6-12 hours.

Pre-cook bacon in microwave until about 1/2 done. (Put two layers of paper towels above and below bacon and cook 2-3 minutes in microwave.)

Brush each piece of meat with brown sugar, then wrap in bacon like a jelly roll. Secure the bacon with toothpicks. A small piece of cheese rolled in is a good complement to these roll ups.

Place on the highest rack in the grill and cook approximately 4-5 minutes on each side, turning only once. Watch them carefully so they don't burn.

Buffalo Pie
By Jen

1 lb ground buffalo meat
2 eggs
2 Tbsp butter
1 cup chopped onion
8 oz egg noodles
3 Tbsp Parmesan cheese
1 jar spaghetti sauce
1/2 cup green peppers
2 cups cottage cheese

Brown the ground buffalo, add onions, peppers, and cook slightly. Add spaghetti sauce.

Cook the egg noodles and drain. Mix the 2 eggs, parmesan cheese and melted butter and coat the noodles. In a 9x13" baking dish, add noodle mixture. spread cottage cheese about 1/2" thick on base of dish. Add buffalo mixture. Top with shredded cheese and bake at 350° for 20 minutes.

Ranae's Venison Stew
By Ranae Edwards

2 lbs venison stew meat cut into 1/2" chunks
5 med potatoes, 1" cubes
1 medium onion, chopped
1 pkg Lipton onion soup mix
1 cup flour
1/4 cup olive oil
1/2 cup fresh carrots
seasoned meat tenderizer
black pepper
1/2 pkg frozen mixed veggies
1 pkg brown gray mix
4 cubes beef bouillon
1/2 cup unsalted butter
1/2 cup chopped celery
2 small cans mushrooms
Mrs Dash seasoning
1/2 cup vinegar

Fill crock pot with 1/2 to 2/3 water and place on high temperature.

Cut up and clean off any white ligaments or fat. Soak venison in 1/2 cup vinegar and 5 cups water for two hours. (Rinse with water and set aside.)

In a bowl, season the venison pieces with seasonings. Pour flour into a ziplock bag and shake to coat. Melt the butter on medium heat in a fry pan and add olive oil. Add flour coated venison and brown. Place the venison, vegetables and remaining ingredients into the crock pot on high until all ingredients start to bubble. Cover and turn heat to low. Cook until all vegetables are done. Cooking time will vary depending on crock pot.

Bison Tenderloin with Lingonberry Glaze
By Karen Wennberg

6 lb bison tenderloin
1 jar Lingonberry preserves or Lingonberry sauce
1 cup diced shallots
1-1/2 to 2 oz red wine vinegar

Sauté shallots with a splash of red wine vinegar until translucent. Add Lingonberry preserves and mix. Coat loin with sauce and place on low heat grill. Baste frequently, cook until internal meat temperature is 140° – 145°. Remove, let rest 10 minutes and cover with more sauce.

BIG GAME RECIPES

Deer Camp Venison Chili
By Brad Gruss

2 lbs ground venison
1/2 lb ground lean pork
1-1/2 Tbsp Worcestershire
1-1/2 Tbsp chili powder
8 oz can stewed tomatoes
1 can chili beans
1 can baked beans
1-1/2 cups chopped green & red peppers
salt and pepper
1/4 cup minced garlic
1 package prepared chili mix

1 lb venison stew meat
1 large onion, chopped
2 Tbsp olive oil
8 oz can tomato juice
2 cups applesauce
1 can pinto beans
1/4 tsp red pepper

1 cup flour
1 juice can water

Dust stew meat with flour and brown in bacon fat or olive oil. Set aside. Cook ground venison and ground pork in remaining bacon grease and/or olive oil. Add chili mix, chili powder, Worcestershire, tomato juice, stewed tomatoes, garlic, green peppers, applesauce and all beans. And remaining spices. Simmer for 1-2 hours. Place in serving bowls and add shredded cheddar cheese to top if desired. Serve with French bread and red wine. Take to deer camp for opening night.

Venison Meat Balls
By Brian Ingals

2 lbs ground venison
1 tsp pepper
pinch of nutmeg
1 egg
2 cups shredded sharp cheddar cheese

2 tsp salt
2 Tbsp dehydrated onion
1/2 cup rolled oats
2 cans cream mushroom soup

Mix all ingredients except soup and cheese. Form meat balls into 1" - 2" balls. Bake meat balls on cookie sheet at 350° for 20 minutes.

In a pan, mix soup and cheese and cook over low to medium heat until well melted. Place all ingredients in a crock pot and heat on low.

Venison Baked Beans
By Will Heinrich

2 lbs ground venison
3/4 cup brown sugar
1 tsp dry mustard
1 lb bacon
1 Vidalia onion
2 Tbsp vinegar
1 cup ketchup
14 oz can tomato soup
salt and pepper to taste
1 Tbsp dark molasses
1 large can baked beans

Cook bacon and cut into 3/4" pieces. Brown ground venison, onions and add bacon. Use a small covered baking dish and add beans, venison mixture, seasonings and soup. Mix well and bake at 350° for 1 hour, or place all ingredients in crock pot and put on low.

Venison/Elk Meatloaf
By Paul and Jessica Zimmerman

1-1/2 lbs ground venison or ground elk
1 medium chopped onion
2 tsp parsley
1 Tbsp Worcestershire
1 egg, beaten
1/4 to 1/2 cup milk
2 tsp garlic powder
salt and pepper to taste
6 oz tomato paste
1/2 can tomato soup

Topping
1/2 cup brown sugar
1/2 cup ketchup or tomato sauce
1 tsp mustard

Combine ground meat, onion, garlic powder, parsley, salt pepper, Worcestershire, tomato paste, beaten egg, soup milk and mix all ingredients. Place in baking dish and add topping. Cook at 350° for 1 hour or until no pink remains.

Moose Stew
By Bob Boren

2 lbs moose stew meat cut into bite size chunks
1 large can stewed tomatoes
4 potatoes cut into 3/4 cubes
1 green peeper, chopped
1/2 tsp celery seed
1 tsp Worcestershire
bacon grease
1 rutabaga or turnip quartered
4 carrots, quartered
2 medium onions
1/4 tsp garlic powder
1 tsp parsley flakes
salt and pepper
cooking oil
4 cups water

Salt, pepper and flour meat cubes. Brown in bacon grease and vegetable oil in Dutch oven or heavy skillet. Add garlic, celery seed, parsley, Worcestershire, green pepper, tomatoes, onion, and 4 cups water. Cover and simmer 1-1/2 hours. Add carrots and rutabaga or turnips. Cook 15 minutes, add potatoes, cook until done, approximately 30-45 minutes.

Venison Stroganoff
By Irene Mortenson and Doris Springer

1 lb venison steak or chops
1-1/2 tsp salt
1 clove garlic
1/2 cup onion chopped
4oz can mushrooms, drained
1 cup sour cream
1 Tbsp Worcestershire
1/2 cup flour
1/4 tsp pepper
1/4 cup butter
3/4 cup water
1 can cream of chicken soup
1 Tbsp catsup

Combine flour, salt pepper, in plastic bag. Add meat and shake well. Melt butter in a large skillet, add meat, garlic and brown. Add onions and continue to brown. Add water and mushrooms and simmer till meat is tender. Add chicken soup, sour cream, catsup 1/2 hour before ready to serve. Alternative method is place all ingredients in crock pot on low for 3-4 hours.

Elk or Venison Meatballs in Cranberry Sauce
By Kevin Fick
(Banquet Fundraiser Chairman for 5 of the 7 to date)

2 lbs ground game
2 eggs
2 Tbsp soy sauce
1/2 tsp pepper

1 cup cornflakes
1/4 cup fresh parsley
1/2 tsp garlic powder

Sauce
16 oz can of whole berry cranberry sauce
1 bottle of chili sauce
2 Tbsp brown sugar
1/2 cup chopped onions
1/2 cup catsup
1 Tbsp lemon juice

Heat oven to 350°. Combine meatball ingredients an a large bowl and mix. Form meat balls into 1-1/2" balls. Place meatballs on a baking dish and bake for 30 minutes at 350° or until meat is not pink. Turn once during baking. Place meatballs in crock pot and mix sauce ingredients. Place sauce in crock pot and heat on low or until sauce is hot and bubbly.

Venison Hot Dish for the Hunting Party
By Earl J. Plattner Sr.

2 lbs ground venison
2 sm cans of mushrooms drained
1 can cream of chicken soup
1 can whole kernel corn
2 Tbsp beef bouillon powder

1 large package egg noodles
1 can cream of mushroom soup
1 can of cream of celery soup
1/2 cup corn flake crumbs
salt and pepper, to taste

Prepare egg noodles according to package directions. When water comes to a boil, add beef bouillon. Brown venison burger and season with salt and pepper to taste. Combine all soups in separate kettle along with corn and mushrooms. Add browned venison burger. Place noodles in very large baking dish and mix in soup venison mixture. Sprinkle top with corn flake crumbs, bake 1 hour at 350° and serve.

BIG GAME RECIPES

Rio Grande Pork or Boar Roast
By Jeremiah Johnson

4-5 lbs roast	1/2 tsp salt
1/2 tsp garlic salt	1/2 tsp chili powder
1 Tbsp vinegar	1/2 cup apple jelly
1/2 cup ketchup	1/2 tsp chili powder
1 cup crusted corn chips	

Preheat oven to 325°. Place pork roast fat side up on rack in a shallow pan. Combine garlic, garlic salt and chili powder and rub ingredients into roast. Place roast in oven for 2 to 2-1/2 hours or until meat temperature is 165°. In a small saucepan combine jelly, ketchup, vinegar, and chili powder. Bring to a boil, reduce heat and simmer uncovered for 2 minutes. Brush glaze on roast, and put corn chips on top. Continue roasting for 10-15 minutes. Remove roast from oven. Take pan drippings and add enough water to make a 1 cup mixture, heat to boiling and pass as meat topping.

Venison Stew
By Grampa Don Lee

1 lb venison steak, cut in 1" cubes
4 Tbsp flour	salt and pepper
1/3 cup olive oil	2 qt water
1/4 cup Worcestershire	4 cloves garlic, crushed

5 carrots, peeled and cut in 1" pieces
5 potatoes, peeled and cut in 1" pieces
1 onion, chopped in large pieces
5 sprigs fresh thyme, strip leaves (or 2 tsp dried thyme)
4 bay leaves

Measure flour into a ziplock bag. Add salt and pepper. Shake bag to coat venison. Add olive oil to an oven proof Dutch oven. (Cast iron works great for this recipe) Dump floured meat into pan and brown. Add water and stir to scrape bottom of pan. Stir in Worcestershire. Add vegetables and herbs. Salt and pepper to taste. Stir to mix.

Bake at 300° for about 5 hours. Meat will be really tender.

Venison Teriyaki Kabobs

By Teri Gruss
(one of our favorites)

1 lb venison filets or medallions

Sauce
1 cup soy sauce
1/2 cup pineapple juice
1 Tbsp garlic powder (not salt)
1/2 cup cider vinegar
1/2 cup brown sugar, pack firmly

Mix sauce ingredients until sugar dissolves. Marinade venison in sauce overnight. Skewer 1" chunks or medallions of venison and grill. This is also a great marinade for goose, pheasant, ribs- any meat, fowl or fish recipe that calls for teriyaki sauce.

Buckshot's Meatballs

By Buckshot Johnson and Lyle & Doris Springer
(Long time local hunter and renowned local chef)

1-1/2 lbs ground game meat
2 Tbsp Worcestershire
1 package onion soup mix
1/2 cup evaporated milk

Sauce
2 cups ketchup
1 cup brown sugar
(Mix ingredients and heat for 10-15 minutes)

Mix all ingredients. Make small meat balls. Put on cookie sheet and bake at 350° for about 15 minutes. Drain and put into sauce. Place all in crock pot on low.

BIG GAME RECIPES

Skewered Venison Steak
By Pam Warnke

2 lbs venison steak cut into 1/2" strips
3/4 cup soy sauce   3/4 cup sugar
3/4 cup beer   3/4 cup semisweet white wine
6 medium garlic cloves, crushed   wooden skewers

Add the beer, wine, soy, sugar and garlic in a bowl and mix until sugar is dissolved. Place venison in bowl, cover and place in refrigerator over night.

Soak wooden skewers in water 2-3 hours. Skewer on meat and grill to medium rare.

Moose Alowettes *(Rolled Moose strips wrapped in bacon)*
By Loreli Westby

1 cup hamburger spice   1 tsp fennel seeds
4 tsp steak pepper   3 tsp black pepper
1 tsp salt   2 lbs. thinly sliced bacon
moose roast (thinly cut into 1/8" slices, as long as bacon strips)

Combine all except bacon and moose with the following
2 tsp season salt   2 tsp onion powder
1 tsp cayenne red pepper

Place pieces of wax paper on cookie sheet. Sprinkle with parsley flakes and then with parmesan cheese. Lay moose slices on top of bacon strips and sprinkle with the spices. Roll strips up and fasten with toothpicks. Freeze for later use or bake at 350° for 30 minutes.

Hungarian Hunters Goulash with Herbed Spaetzle

By Chef Dawn Savoie (New Orleans, Louisiana) Serves 6-8

3 lbs venison, elk or moose tips
4 fl oz of lard or vegetable oil
6 large onions
1/2 cup sweet or smoked paprika
2 qts chicken or vegetable Stock
1/2 tsp caraway seed
4 lbs mushrooms
1/4 cup hot paprika
1/4 cup tomato paste

Salt and pepper the meat and sear in a very hot pan in 2 fl oz of lard or vegetable oil until browned. Do not cook the meat all the way through. Remove meat from pan and set aside. Discard oil from pan and add about a cup of water to remove meat sucs from pan bottom. Reserve the liquid. In another sauce pan, sauté onions and mushrooms until lightly browned. You may have to do this in small batches to prevent over crowding pan and to ensure vegetables get nicely browned. Once vegetables are sautéed, add the paprikas and tomato paste. Stir until paste is fully incorporated. Return the meat, along with the reserved liquid, back to the pan and add the chicken/vegetable stock and caraway seed. Cover and cook on med–low until the meat is very tender and sauce nicely thickened. Serve with Herbed Spaetzle.

Venison Dill Roast

By Loreli Westby

1 venison roast
32 oz jar of whole, large, dill pickles

Place roast in crock pot. Pour the jar of pickles and juice over the roast. Cook on low heat for 8 hours.

BIG GAME RECIPES

Herbed Spaetzle

3 cups all purpose flour
3/4 cup whole milk
1/4 tsp nutmeg
1/2 Tbsp fresh thyme
6-8 oz sour cream (1 oz per serving, stirred into dish)

6 eggs
salt and pepper, to taste
1/4 cup fresh parsley

Mound the flour like a well. Mix the eggs by hand until well blended. Add the milk to thin the batter. The batter should be smooth and gooey. Add the nutmeg, herbs and salt and pepper. Cover and let rest for one hour.

To cook spaetzle, place the batter in a perforated pan or colander suspended over a large pot of boiling water. With a bowl scraper, push the batter through the holes, allowing the batter to fall into the boiling water. You must work very fast or else the batter will begin to cook in the colander making it hard to push through. Lower the water to a simmer and allow the spaetzel to cook until they float to the surface. This will take 3–4 minutes. Strain the spaetzle and place in an ice bath to stop the cooking process. Once cooled, remove spaetzle from ice bath and hold until ready to cook. When ready to serve, heat a sauté pan with butter and sauté spaetzle until lightly browned. Season with salt and pepper and serve along side the stew.

Ross's Canadian Moose Meatballs

By Ross Pearson

5 lbs ground moose meat
1 cup milk
4 eggs
salt, pepper, garlic powder (to taste)

2 lbs Italian spicy sausage
2 cups bread crumbs
1/4 cup crushed fresh garlic

Mix all ingredients and make 1-1/4" balls. Place meatballs on a cookie sheet and bake at 375° for 15-20 minutes or until crispy brown on outside.

Make homemade brown gravy from remaining oil off of cookie pan.

Put meatballs in a casserole dish, cover with gravy and bake at 350° 45-60 minutes.

Venison Rendang
By Chef Charlie Gruss

2 lbs venison stew meat (1" cubes, preferably from the chuck)
1 6-8 oz can of coconut milk
1/4 cup coconut flakes (toasted and ground)
1/3 tsp coriander seed (ground)

2 shallots (thinly sliced)	1 clove garlic (minced, pasted)
1 - 1" piece ginger (minced)	1 tsp curry powder
1 stalk lemongrass (cleaned, thinly sliced)	
1 tsp fresh mint (minced)	2 Tbsp cilantro (minced)
1 tsp Sriracha Sauce	

Heat oil in a large stew pot. In small batches, sear the venison, reserve seared meat in a separate container. Repeat until all the meat is seared. Add all the meat back to the stew pot and add in the coconut milk, bring to a simmer and cook for 2 hours on a low simmer. Toast coconut flakes and coriander in a sauté pan and once cooled, grind in a clean coffee grinder until you have a fine powder, add into stew. Sauté the shallots until lightly caramelized and add to stew. Sauté garlic, lemongrass, ginger, and curry powder until they aromatize. Add herbs and Sriracha sauce then pour in all ingredients to your stew. Continue on a low simmer until all the flavors blend. Taste and adjust salt content.

Control Points
It is very important to not overcrowd your pan when searing the meat. If there is not enough space between meat cubes you will achieve steaming not searing and not develop the flavor base caused by the Maillard Reaction when meat is browned or caramelized.

Venison Tid Bits

By Chef Marcus Hamblett (New England Culinary Institute Instructor)

Marinate for a day, desired amount of venison tenderloin cut into small bite size pieces

1/3 cup red wine	6 Tbsp soy sauce
1 tsp thyme	1 head whole garlic cut in 1/4s
1 tea rosemary	1/2 small onion
1 cup oil	1/2 lb bacon

Shake all ingredients (except bacon) in ziplock bag and let sit for 24 hours. Take out of marinade and pat dry. Wrap a small piece of bacon around chunk of meat. Set oven to broil, put meat on a skewer and place on broiler rack or sheet pan and place in oven. Cook on lowest rack possible, then move closer to top for a crisper finish.

Chapter 7
Upland Bird Recipes

Stewed Fricassee of Pheasant

By Thelma Clark

2 pheasants cut in 4-6 pieces each
flour
1/2 stick butter
pinch Lawry's salt
2 capfuls Worcestershire
4 cloves minced fresh garlic
garlic pepper
tarragon (mass quantities)
salt and pepper
2 cups of cream
1/4 cup sweet vermouth
1 medium chopped onion
rosemary to taste
fresh mushrooms, sliced

Roll pheasants in flour seasoned with salt and pepper. Brown thoroughly in butter in large skillet. Add cream and remainder of above. Set on back of stove, covered, to simmer about 1 hour. Taste for seasoning. Serve over noodles.

Pheasant

By Shirley Skauge

9x13" baking pan
1 small bottle French dressing
1 package dry onion soup mix
1/2 cup water.
4-8 pheasant breasts
1/3 jar orange marmalade

Marinate breasts for 1 hour from the ingredients above. Turn at least once. Bake at 350° for 1 to 1-1/2 hours.

Chow Mein with Pheasant
By Chuck "Buckshot" Johnson

4 pheasant legs and 4 pheasant thighs
1/4 cup salad oil
4 cups chopped celery
1 can bean sprouts
1 can mushrooms
1/4 cup soy sauce
salt and pepper
2 large onions chopped
1 cup water
2-1/2 Tbsp cornstarch

Parboil legs and thighs in water and then remove meat from bones and tendons, set aside.

Heat oil and salt and pepper. Add celery, onions, bean sprout juice and 1 cup water. Cook until celery is tender. Add sprouts and mushrooms. Mix cornstarch, 1/4 cup water and soy sauce. Stir until thick, then add pheasant pieces.

Pheasant Tortillas
By Gwen Lillemon
(this is a good one too!)

8 oz shredded Cheddar Jack cheese
1 can cream of mushroom soup
1/2 cup green peppers
1/2 cup chopped onions
1-1/2 cups chicken broth
1 can cream of chicken soup
1/4 cup Jalapeño peppers
1 bag tortillas

Place clean birds in crock pot with 1/2 volume of water. Cover and put on high–medium for 6-8 hours. Allow to cool and then de-bone pheasants and shred meat. Butter bottom and sides of 9x13" baking dish. Add a layer of tortillas. Mix the meat with soups, peppers, onions. Place a layer of meat mixture, then a cheese layer. Repeat two times with cheese on top. Bake at 350° for 20-30 minutes. Cool 10 minutes. Cut and serve.

Pheasant Enchiladas
By Rick Thiery

1 pheasant, cooked and shredded (about 3 cups)
1 medium onion diced
1 can cream of mushroom soup
1 pint sour cream
corn or flour tortillas
1 can enchilada sauce
16 oz cheddar cheese

Mix meat together with onions, soup and sour cream. Put small amount of enchilada sauce in the bottom of a 9x13" baking dish. Spoon meat mixture into tortillas and roll up. Place tortillas into pan, pour remaining sauce over tortillas and top with cheddar cheese. Bake 1 hour at 350°. Serve with lettuce, salsa and sour cream.

Pleasant Pheasant Egg Rolls
By Ranae Edwards

1-2 pheasant breasts de-boned and ground
2 cups fresh sliced mushrooms
1 pkg coleslaw mix (chopped cabbage and carrots)
2 chopped green onions or 1/4 cup regular onions
2/3 cup chopped celery
ground ginger to taste (approx. 1 tsp)
sea salt to taste (approx. 1 tsp)   3 Tbsp soy sauce
1 pkg Melissa's egg roll wrap   1 egg
unsalted butter and olive oil   canola oil

Beat egg and two tablespoons of water for roll wrapping edge sealing. In a skillet heat equal parts of butter and olive oil, approximately 2-3 tablespoons each. When hot, fry pheasant until brown and set aside. Heat additional equal parts of oil and butter and add coleslaw mix and fry until tender/crisp. Fry the mushrooms, celery, onions until tender/crisp and set aside. Mix all the ingredients together with soy sauce, ginger and salt and fry.

Spoon about 1/2 cup veggie and pheasant mixture into each square egg roll wrap. Follow wrapping instructions on the egg roll package, using the egg/water mixture to seal the edges. Place the egg rolls in a hot skillet with canola oil and fry till light golden. Enjoy.

Pheasant Pot Pie

By Rick Wilcox

2 lbs cooked cubed pheasant meat
2 Tbsp oil
1/2 tsp salt
1/4 tsp black pepper
1 can cream of chicken soup
1 pre-made pie crust
2 Tbsp butter
1/2 tsp thyme
1 pkg 16 oz mixed vegetables
1/2 cup white wine or milk

In a 10-inch oven-proof skillet add oil and heat med-high. Add pheasant, salt, thyme, pepper and cook 2 minutes stirring frequently. Reduce heat to medium and add vegetables, soup, wine, and simmer 5 minutes.

Add pie crust to top and make slits to vent. Bake at 425° for 45 minutes or until crust is done

Pheasant Pie

By Glen Bean   Serves 4-6

Boil one pheasant, until tender, with one onion, two leafstalks of celery, and salt/pepper to taste. When tender, remove meat from bone and dice. Strain and reserve 3 cups broth.

Dice one onion, and some celery. Sauté in 1 Tbsp butter, until tender but NOT brown (add mushrooms, to enhance flavor).

Melt 1/2 stick butter, and stir in 3 Tbsp flour. Add strained broth, brought to a boil, previously. Stir until smooth. Remove from heat. Add a little white wine, Worcestershire and a mix of basil, marjoram, thyme, and tarragon to taste. Add sautéed onion, celery, mushroom.

Place pheasant meat in casserole dish/pie plate, pour in thickened stock, and cover with pie crust.

Bake at 450° until pie crust is done and brown.

UPLAND BIRD RECIPES

Pheasant Fingers
By Ottertail County Pheasants Forever
(You can go through a lot of pheasant with this one)

2 de-boned pheasant breasts, cut into 2" strips
1 bottle 3 oz of Crystal hot sauce
2 Tbsp melted butter
1 tsp white vinegar
1 packet 7 oz dry Italian salad dressing
3/4 cup flour, seasoned with cayenne pepper
canola oil for frying

Dip
Prepare Blue cheese salad dressing or sour cream mixed with hot sauce, to taste.

In medium, non-metallic mixing bowl combine hot sauce, melted butter, vinegar and salad dressing mix. Add pheasant pieces and blend well. Let sit at room temperature for at least 45 minutes or for 3 hours in refrigerator (the longer you marinate, the hotter/spicier the bits will be). Place seasoned flour in plastic bag, drop in a few pieces of pheasant and coat with flour mixture. Set aside and repeat until all pheasant is coated. Heat the oil and fry pheasant pieces till brown.

Pheasant Cordon Bleu
By Rick Thiery

boneless skinned pheasant breasts
egg wash   cracker bread crumb mixture
slices, Swiss cheese   ham slices

Clean and dry pheasant breasts, dip in egg wash and coat in crushed cracker crumbs. Cover each breast with a slice of Swiss cheese. Place in oven at 350° for 30 minutes. Remove from oven and place a slice of ham over cheese and add one more slice of Swiss on top. Cover pan and bake in oven for 10-15 minutes until cheese is melted and ham is warm.

Pheasant with Creamy Wine Sauce
By Jill Ingals

1 pheasant, cleaned and de-boned, cut into bite size pieces
1 cup flour
1/2 cup olive oil
1-1/2 cups heavy cream
Pinch dried thyme
salt and pepper
1 small onion diced
6 oz dry white wine
1 cup chicken stock

Heat oven to 350°. Season pheasant pieces with salt and pepper. Dredge pieces in flour. Heat oil over medium-high heat in heavy cast iron skillet. Brown pheasant pieces on both sides. Remove excess oil from pan and sauté onion for 2 minutes. Put pheasant pieces back into pan, add chicken stock. Cover and bake for 1-1/2 hours. Add cream, wine, thyme and 1 tsp salt. Bake approximately 1 more hour. Season to taste with salt and pepper. Serve over rice or egg noodles.

Braised Game Birds, Rabbit or Squirrel
By Banquet Attendee 05

2-3 lbs of game bird, rabbit or squirrel cut into 6-8 pieces
2 Tbsp olive oil
5 Tbsp flour
2 Tbsp unsalted butter
1/4 cup dry white wine
1 large onion cut into 8 pieces
1 tsp coarse salt
1 cup homemade chicken stock
1/2 lb mushrooms
1 tsp chopped fresh thyme or rosemary
chopped fresh parsley

Heat the olive oil in a large skillet over medium-high heat. Add onions and sauté until golden brown, about 8 minutes. Transfer onions to a bowl and set aside. In a shallow bowl, stir flour and salt together and dredge the meat pieces in the mixture. Melt 1 Tbsp of butter, add the meat and sauté until lightly browned. Layer the onion over the top and pour in the chicken stock, white wine and thyme/rosemary. Cover and simmer 30-40 minutes or until tender.

UPLAND BIRD RECIPES

Crock Pot Pheasant

By Duke Anderson
(50 year Guide on Lake Christina)

2 pheasants, cleaned and rinsed well
1 can cream of mushroom soup
1 can cream of chicken soup
1/2 cup sweet Vermouth
1 large onion sliced
1/2 lb sour cream
1 cup raisins
1 cup dried tomatoes
2 cups sliced mushrooms

Cut pheasants in half. Place dried tomatoes into sweet vermouth and soak for 45 minutes. Add all ingredients into crock pot. Set on low and cook all day.

Battered Fried Baked Pheasant

By Lyman Wild Game Cookbook

1 pheasant, cut up
2 eggs
1 can mushroom soup
1/2 soup can of water
salt and pepper
2 Tbsp water
flour
1 cup fine bread crumbs
vegetable oil

Beat eggs and water well and refrigerate until ready to use.

Dip pheasant pieces into batter and roll in flour. Dip in batter again and roll in bread crumbs. Refrigerate pheasant for 2 hours before frying. Pour oil in electric fryer about 1/2" thick. Heat to 375° and fry pheasant until well browned but not done. Salt and pepper after frying and place in casserole dish. Dilute mushroom soup with water and pour over bird. Cover and bake at 350° for 1 hour.

Horseradish Pheasant Casserole
By Dave "160K" Kokenberger

2 cups chicken stock
1 med onion, chopped
Season salt
1 qt whipping cream
1 cup Mozzarella cheese

2–5 oz jars prepared horseradish
1 large garlic bulb, crushed
Cracked black pepper
2 cups chopped mushrooms
1 cup Swiss cheese

Quarter pheasants, dust with flour and brown in butter. Place in roaster.

Add stock, garlic, onion, mushrooms, horseradish, seasonings and cheese.

Bake at 300° for 30-45 minutes. Let rest 15 minutes. If necessary, thicken with flour/cold water paste by gently stirring in. Add whipping cream mix and serve over rice or noodles.

Iowegin Pheasant
By Gene Gerdes

2 pheasants, deboned
1 medium onion
1/4 lb butter
2 cans cream of celery soup
Bay leaf
1 can dried onion rings

1/2 lb fresh mushrooms
1/4 cup chopped garlic
4 oz cream
2 oz Brandy
3 cups broken potato chips
salt and pepper

Cut pheasant into bite size pieces. Brown in butter, set aside. Sauté garlic, onion and mushrooms in remaining butter. Pour off butter and add all ingredients into baking dish. Add pheasant, and mix. Place potato chips on top of mixture, add dried onion rings on top of chips. Bake at 350° for 30-40 minutes.

Pheasant Breasts
By Buckshot Johnson

2 pheasant breasts
butter
garlic salt
fresh mushrooms

flour
2 cans mushroom soup
1 lb sour cream

Remove breast meat from the bones. Flour and brown in large frying pan with butter and garlic salt. Sauté fresh mushrooms in pan. Add mushroom soup and bake in oven for 1-1/2 hours at 350°. Add the sour cream 20 minutes before serving. Pour gravy over baked potato.

Creamy Pheasant Stew with Dumplings
By Banquet Attendee 07

1 pheasant breast, cut into small chunks
2 Tbsp butter
1 egg
1 cup flour
1/4 cup white cooking wine
1 celery stalk diced
1-1/2 cups baby carrots sliced
Water or canned chicken bullion

2 Tbsp olive oil
1/2 cup milk
1 lg can cream of chicken soup
2 potatoes peeled and diced
1/2 small onion chopped
olive oil for frying

Dip pheasant pieces into egg/milk wash mixture, then dust with flour. Fry in olive oil until lightly browned. Place the fried pheasant, all vegetables, soup and wine into slow cooker on high for about 1 hour.

Baking Powder Biscuits

1-1/2 cups all purpose flour
1 tsp salt
1/4 cup softened butter

2 tsp baking powder
1 tsp tarragon
3/4 cup milk

In a bowl combine flour, baking powder, salt and tarragon. Add butter and toss to make a crumbly mixture. Add milk and stir gently to make dough. (do not over stir) Make sure there are no dry flour clumps. Drop by using teaspoon into bubbling stew. Cover and simmer for 10 minutes or until done.

Oh Shit, That's Good Pheasant
By Roger Dalum

1-2 pheasants
1 bottle beer
salt and pepper, to taste
3-6 cloves garlic, minced
1/2 - 1 cup flour
1/2 cup olive oil

De-bone breasts and thighs, pound to no more than 1/2" thick.

Dip pheasant pieces in beer, roll in flour. Pan fry in olive oil until browned.

Pour about 1/4 of olive oil in a roasting pan, add browned pheasant and roast for 1 hour at 350°. Add minced garlic (3 to 4 cloves for one pheasant, more if cooking two pheasants).

Add 1" of water to the roasting pan and return to oven. Check after about 30 minutes. Don't let the pan dry out. Add more water if needed.

Pheasant in Mushroom Wild Rice
By Scott Wisgerhoff

2-3 cups cooked pheasant, shredded
3 cups chicken stock
2 cups fresh mushroom (8 oz)
1 cup uncooked wild rice
1/2 cup sunflower seeds
2 bay leaves
2 cans cream of celery soup
1/2 cup uncooked white rice
1 cup diced red onion
1 Tbsp Worcestershire
1/2 tsp black pepper

Place all ingredients into crock pot. Cook on high for approximately 3 hours or until rice is cooked. Remove the bay leaves. This recipe is good for using leg and thigh meat, although tedious to cook and de-bone.

Pheasant & Spinach Manicotti
By Kevin Fick

1 whole dressed pheasant

Boil pheasant in water with 1 onion, 1-1/2 cups chopped carrots, 4 cloves garlic chopped, 2 celery stalks cut, salt, pepper, 2 bay leaves, for 1 hour or done.

Save stock for soup, retain 1-2 cups for recipe. Cube pheasant breast into 1/4" to 1/2" pieces.

5 oz frozen spinach	3 Tbsp butter
3 Tbsp flour	1-2 cups pheasant stock
1/2 cup milk	3 – 8-oz cans tomato sauce
2 tsp basil	2 tsp oregano
2 tsp garlic powder	1 tsp brown sugar
2 cups Monterey Jack cheese	1 cup Ricotta cheese
6 manicotti shells, large	

Allow spinach to thaw and dry with paper towels. Place spinach in a bowl with the diced pheasant. In a large sauce pan, melt butter, and flour while mixing over med-high heat. Gradually add broth, and milk and cook until thickened. Stir in tomato sauce, basil, oregano, garlic powder and brown sugar. Reduce to medium heat. Stuff pheasant, spinach, 1/2 cup Monterey Jack cheese and 1/2 cup Ricotta into each manicotti shell. Grease a 9x13" baking dish, pour 1/2" of tomato mixture into dish. Set in or arrange manicotti shells in the dish. Pour remaining sauce over the top, add remaining cheese to top. Bake at 350° for 45 minutes. Let stand 5 minutes before serving.

Braised Pheasant

By Chef Charlie Gruss Serves 4

4 pheasants (split along breastbone)
1/4 lb unsalted butter, (large dice and kept cold)
3 cup white button mushrooms (sliced)
1 cup white table wine   1 cup poultry stock
1/2 lemon (juiced)   2 cup pearl onions
1 tsp Kosher salt   1 tsp fresh ground black pepper
2 Tbsp oil

Heat a braising pan on medium-high heat, add oil. Season pheasants with salt and sear so as much of the outside skin as possible is golden brown. Remove pheasants from pan and add sliced mushrooms and pearl onions, Sauté until caramelized. Deglaze pan with white wine and lemon juice, stirring the pan with a wooden spoon to release the sucs (browned bits) from the bottom. Add the pheasants back and bring liquid to a simmer. Cover and cook approximately 1 hour. Remove pheasant from braising liquid and whisk in cold pieces of butter. Taste and adjust seasonings.

Control Points

1. Do not season the braising liquid until the pheasants are cooked, taken out, and the butter has been incorporated. When braising, your liquid will reduce and condense any flavors within. So, if you season the liquid beforehand, your braising liquid will be overly salty.

2. A good sear of the pheasants is very important to building flavor in this dish.

Grandma LaVette's Roast Pheasant
By Paulette Dalum

2 pheasants (thighs and breasts. fileted)
1/2 can beer
1 Tbsp Lawry's season salt
1/3 cup onion, minced fine
1-1/2 cups flour
6 cloves garlic, minced fine
olive oil for frying

Preheat oven to 350°. Dip breasts and thighs in beer to wet and roll in flour until fully covered. Pan fry in extra virgin olive oil until well browned. Place pheasant in roasting pan, layer if necessary. Sprinkle season salt on top. Add water to fill 1/2" of roasting pan.

Bake at 350° for 1 hour. Check at 30 minutes to make sure you have water in pan.

Creamed Fillet of Turkey/Pheasant
By Priscilla Reineke

bag of flour
1 turkey breast, or 1 pheasant
pinch of salt and pepper
1 pint of heavy whipping cream

Debone turkey/pheasant and cut into bite-size pieces. Shake pieces in bag of flour, salt & pepper and season to taste. Brown pieces in fry pan. Place in shallow baking pan. Pour container of whipping cream over top and cover with tinfoil. Bake approx.. 1 hour at 325°-350°. Check and bake 15-20 minutes uncovered.

Baroque Pheasant Breast

By Mel Bois

2 pheasant breast, split into four parts
sliced mozzarella cheese
1 large can of sliced (not chunks) pineapple
barbecue sauce (sweet is better)
toothpicks

All cooking will be done on a Weber gas-type grill (indirect heat is a must since pheasant dries out easily). The hood should be closed at all times unless adding to the dish or checking. High indirect heat is needed

Drain the juice from the pineapple into a separate container. Split the pheasant breasts into four parts. Rinse and dry. Marinate the breast in the pineapple juice for about 1 hour.

Heat the grill with all burners at high. Cut the breast into a butterfly cut, not cutting all the way through the breast. Turn the center burner off. Place the butterfly down on the center of the grill for 2 minutes. Baste with sauce. Cover the grill. Flip the breasts with one side down. Cook for 3 - 4 minutes. Baste once again. Cover the grill. Flip the breast one more time. Baste one last time. Cover the grill. Place 2 slices of pineapple on each breast. Cover with a slice of mozzarella cheese. Hold in place with toothpicks. Cover the grill. Check the breasts until they are cooked to your liking. Place a third slice of pineapple on the breast. Hold in place with toothpicks. Cover with barbecue sauce. Continue to grill until the sauce is hot. Remove and serve.

Pulled Turkey Breast Sandwiches
By Tiffany Reineke

2 turkey breasts
2 cups water (enough to just cover breasts in roaster)
1 tsp garlic powder
1 Tbsp McCormick Grillmates Montreal Steak
    (or similar seasoning)

Cook turkey breasts in roaster for 5 hours at 325° (checking water occasionally so it doesn't dry out). Shred turkey into crock pot, keeping liquid from roaster. Add seasoning and warm on low, serve with buns.

Chapter 8
Fish Recipes

FISH RECIPES

Pistachio Nut Crusted Walleye
By Pam Warnke

2-4 8-oz walleye fillets
4 Tbsp olive oil
4 Tbsp butter
pinch ground pepper
1/2 tsp salt
1-1/2 cups bread crumbs

1 cup flour
2 eggs, beaten
2 Tbsp milk
pinch cayenne pepper
1-1/2 cups pistachios, chopped

In a bowl, whip eggs and milk. In a separate bowl add and mix bread crumbs and pistachio nuts, salt and pepper. Dust fillets in flour, shake off excess and dredge in egg wash. Roll in pistachio nuts and bread-crumb mixture.

In a large skillet over medium-high heat add butter and oil and brown filets each side for 3-4 minutes until crispy brown.

Boiled Lake Trout
By Shane at Lost Island Lodge & Fremont Gruss Jr.

1 – 4-6 lb lake trout
4 quarts water
1 cup salt
melted butter

Clean the trout, remove head, tail and fins. Starting at the top of the neck, cut from top down to belly meat, in approximately 2" strips.

Boil the water and add salt. Immerse the trout strips into the boiling salt water mixture for 12-15 minutes. Make sure the water is boiling when you remove the fish. Remove skin from meat. Dip in melted butter and enjoy the poor man's lobster.

Donn's Fish Chowder

By Donn Vellekson

4-5 lbs of northern pike
3 med carrots, chopped
3-4 celery stalks, chopped
4 med potatoes, cubed
1 med onion, sliced
1/2 tsp fresh ginger
salt and pepper, to taste

12 oz can chicken broth
1/4 cup sherry or white wine
1 tsp fresh garlic
2-3 Tbsp clam juice
3 dried bay leaves
1-1/2 pints half & half

Place all ingredients (except half & half and fish) in Dutch oven. Cover and simmer over medium heat. During this time, place fish in steam basket over other ingredients and steam until done (about 10 minutes) Remove fish and de-bone.

After vegetables are fully cooked (about 45 minutes), remove bay leaves and add fish and half & half. Return to simmer for 10 minutes and serve. (Even better next day!)

Fish Cakes

By Paulette Dalum

3 cups northern fillet, frozen
1 small chopped onion
salt and pepper to taste

cooked mashed potatoes
1 egg

Grind northern while semi-frozen, using coarse blade. Small bones will be chopped up and not noticeable. For every 3 cups of ground fish add 1/2 cup mashed potatoes. Add egg, onion salt and pepper. Use large ice cream scoop for size of patty. Fry patties in 1" of hot oil or until golden brown on each side.

FISH RECIPES

Fish Patties
By Brent Olson

2 lbs northern pike
1 medium onion
1 tsp salt

1 lb raw potatoes
2 eggs
1 tsp pepper

Grind fish in a coarse grind blend. Grind raw potatoes and onion. Mix fish, potatoes and onions. Add salt and pepper. Add two eggs and mix thoroughly Make patties about 1/4 pound each. Pre-heat cast iron skillet to med-high 350° – 375°. Fry until golden brown. Turn and fry other side.

Walleye on a Stick
By Outdoors Weekly / Banquet Attendee 07

2 lbs walleye fillets
red, green, yellow peppers
1/4 cup honey
1 Tbsp Cajun seasoning
salt and pepper, to taste

2 Tbsp teriyaki sauce
small whole onions
2 Tbsp soy sauce
1/2 tsp Worcestershire

Mix honey, soy sauce, teriyaki, Cajun, Worcestershire. Add salt and pepper to taste. Cut walleye, peppers and onions into 1" - 2" pieces. Lay walleye, peppers, and onion in Tupperware container and cover with honey mixture overnight in refrigerator. Alternate fish, peppers onion on skewers. Grill and enjoy!

Beer Batter for Deep Frying
By Karen Wenberg

1/2 cup white flour
salt and pepper
paprika

1/2 cup wheat flour
garlic and onion powder
1 egg

Mix together in a ziplock bag. Beat 1 egg into bowl and add 10 oz of a heavy dark beer like a stout! Mix with egg to blend. Prepare hot oil in fryer. Dredge fish in egg wash and put few fish pieces into ziplock bag and shake to coat. Cook in oil to golden brown.

Lake Trout in Asparagus Sauce
By Lyman Fish Cookery

2 lbs winter-caught lake trout, skinned
1/2 cup cream
1 cup asparagus sauce
1/2 cup grated cheddar cheese
1/2 cup prepared French-style mustard
salt and pepper
1/2 cup white wine

Wipe the fillets with a damp cloth, cut into serving portions. Season the fish with salt and pepper. Sauté quickly on each side. Place in the bottom of a well-buttered glass baking pan.

Deglaze the sauté pan with the wine and mix in mustard. Blend in cream and asparagus sauce. Pour over fish. Bake in a pre-heated hot oven (400°) for about 20 minutes, or until bubbly and the fish is cooked. Sprinkle cheese over top and return to oven until cheese has melted.

Serve with fresh cooked asparagus tips, dressed with hot lemon butter.

This recipe also works well with walleye, sauger or any white fleshed fish.

FISH RECIPES

Stuffed Fillets of Largemouth Bass
By J. Thompson

1-1/2 to 2 lbs bass filets
1 Tbsp butter
1/4 cup minced onion
slices stale bread
1/2 cup milk
oil for frying
1/4 tsp thyme
1 egg, beaten
flour
1 egg yolk, beaten
1/2 cup fine, dry bread crumbs

Wipe the fillets with a damp cloth.

Melt the butter and cook the onion until translucent. Soak the bread in the milk until soft and wet, and squeeze dry, rubbing and crumbling the bread with your hands. Mix the bread with the onion, add seasonings, and mix with the beaten egg to bind. Divide the mixture evenly, spread it over the fillets and roll up the fish, fastening with a toothpick. Dust the roll ups with flour, dip in beaten egg yolk, and roll in bread crumbs. Arrange in deep fat fryer basket. Fry until golden brown, remove tooth picks. Serve with tomato dipping sauce.

Broiled Walleye Fillets
By Ken Marquis

2 – 2 lb walleye fillets, skinned and washed
3-4 scallions
1/2 tsp lemon juice
1/2 cup Parmesan cheese
4 Tbsp mayonnaise
fresh ground pepper
3 Tbsp butter

Take 4 fillets and place in buttered roasting pan. Broil for 2-3 minutes. Gently turn fillets over. Take all other ingredients, mix together well and spread on filets. Broil again for 2-3 minutes.

Walleye Piccata with Caper Thyme Buerre Blanc Sauce"

By Chef Charlie Gruss Serves 4

1 Tbsp white wine
1/8 cup heavy cream
1 shallot (small dice)
2 sprigs thyme (minced)
1 lb unsalted butter (large dice and kept cold until use)
4 Tbsp white wine vinegar
3/4 tsp salt
2 Tbsp capers

Combine white wine, white wine vinegar, salt, thyme and shallot. Reduce on high heat until all liquid is almost gone. Turn heat down to medium and add heavy cream. Reduce by half. Slowly add butter 1 piece at a time while whisking to form an emulsion. Wait to add each additional piece of butter until the first is melted and whisked in, whisk constantly. Finish with capers and taste to recheck seasoning. Add more salt at this time if desired. If desired you could substitute the juice of 1 lemon for the white wine vinegar for your acid.

Control Points
1. Heat should not exceed 136° when incorporating butter or the sauce will break.
2. Heavy cream adds Emulsion Insurance to this sauce.
3. Use a non-aluminum pan; aluminum will discolor sauce, turning it grey.
4. Hold sauce in a warm area and serve as quickly as possible.

Walleye

By Chef Charlie Gruss

4 fillets from 1-1/2 to 2 lb walleyes
1 cup all-purpose flour
1 Tbsp fresh ground black pepper
1/8 cup water
1 Tbsp Kosher salt
3 eggs (beaten)
2 Tbsp peanut oil

Clean walleye and de-skin. Mix flour, salt and fresh ground black pepper, in a baking dish large enough for the fillets. Beat eggs with water. Pat dry walleye fillets and season with salt and black pepper. Place fillets in flour mixture and shake off excess. Do all the fillets and let rest for 1-2 minutes, this will help the flour adhere.

Heat a large sauté pan coated with a thin layer of peanut oil on medium-high heat. Place fillets in the egg wash to coat entirely and place directly into hot sauté pan. Cook each side 3-4 minutes until golden brown. Remove and lightly re-season with salt.

Control Points
Heat control of the pan is the most important element to this dish. If the pan is too hot you will burn the egg flour coating.

Jamaican Pike Eskevechie

By Donald "Prento" Allen
(This is special, if you like spicy and a hint of vinegar)

3 lbs northern pike fillets, cut into 2"x4" strips
3 large Vidalia onions, sliced
1 yellow pepper
1-2 Scotch Bonnet "hot" peppers
Jamaican spice / Cajun spice
virgin coconut oil
1 large green pepper
1 red pepper
Old Bay seasoning
3 cups white vinegar

Rinse the skinless fish fillets and lay on paper towels. Liberally apply Old Bay seasoning on one side. Turn over and liberally apply Jamaican spice (Cajun spice can be used) to the other side. Refrigerate for 1-3 hours.

Quarter and slice peppers, slice onions and carefully (using rubber gloves) separate the Scotch Bonnet meat from the seeds. Chop pepper into fine pieces. The amount of "heat"/ spiciness is dependent on the pepper strength and amount used!

Pre-heat the coconut oil. Take fish out and cut into 2-4 oz portions. Deep fry the fish in hot oil for 3-5 minutes. Remove fish and set on platter. Carefully add 2 cups of white vinegar to the oil, add peppers, onion and scotch bonnet. Cook and stir the peppers until done but crisp. Ladle out the vegetables, place on serving tray and top off with the fish fillets. Serve hot.

FISH RECIPES

Deviled Perch Fillets
By Timothy Manion, Game and Fish Cookbook

16 perch fillets
1/2 cup Worcestershire
1/4 cup steak sauce
1/4 tsp cayenne
1 tsp black pepper
1/4 cup softened butter

juice of 3 lemons
1/2 cup chili sauce
1 tsp dry mustard
1 cup buttered bread crumbs
salt to taste

Preheat oven to 425°. Mix Worcestershire, lemon juice, steak sauce, chili sauce. cayenne, mustard and black pepper. Spread on fillets and let stand for 1/2 hour. Place fillets in greased baking dish and bake at 425° for 20 minutes. A few minutes before done, add salt to taste. Remove from oven, sprinkle with buttered crumbs, drizzle with butter and place under broiler to brown.

Fish Soup ala Eagles Nest
By Buzz & Suz Fritch

1 medium potato
1 small onion
1 bay leaf
1 tsp Old Bay seasoning
1 cup cubed fish (northern or sunfish)

1 carrot
1 tomato bullion cube
1 tsp oregano
1-1/2 Tbsp olive oil

Sauté everything except fish for a little while then add 3 cups water and simmer till veggies are tender. Add cubed fish and simmer until fish is cooked. This recipe is guaranteed to improve your aim during duck season!

Finnish-style Fish Soup
By Hilja Tapanaineu & Lyman Fish Cookery

1 lb of perch or northern pike fillets
2 cups water
3 medium potatoes
1 tsp flour
2 cups milk
1/4 medium onion
1/2 tsp salt
7 whole peppercorns
1 Tbsp. butter

Boil potatoes in water for about 10 minutes. Add the fish, peppercorns, onion and salt. Cook until potatoes are done.

Add flour to milk and mix well. Add the milk to the soup, stirring while it heats, then blend in the butter. Let the soup cook for about 3 minutes and it is ready to serve.

Beer Batter Trout
By Sandra Beitzel

1 cup all purpose flour
1 tsp baking powder
1 tsp red pepper
2 lbs trout filet
1 cup cornstarch
1 tsp sugar
1 12-oz bottle of beer
oil for frying

Combine flour, cornstarch, baking powder, sugar and red pepper in bowl. Add beer and mix well. Cut fish into 1" strips. Dip in batter and fry in hot oil.

FISH RECIPES

Camp Fish Fry
By Doug Alexander

Fish fillets with skin on
fresh lemon juice
salt and pepper

butter
garlic salt

Arrange fish fillets, skin side down, on a sheet of aluminum foil. Place on grill over hot coals. Brush on equal parts of butter and lemon juice seasoned with garlic, salt and pepper. Grill uncovered, just until fish begins to flake, do not over cook! Remove from foil with spatula; skin will stick to foil.

Almond Crusted Walleye
By Chef Matt Annand

6-8 oz walleye fillets
1 cup medium coarse pressed bread crumbs
salt
2 eggs, whipped
olive oil for sautéing

flour
1 cup crushed almonds

Sauce
1/4 cup butter
fresh bay leaves

1/4 cup golden raisins
1/2 lemon, juiced

In a hot pan add 1 tsp butter. As soon as the butter melts add the raisins and bay leaves. When butter reaches golden brown and starts to foam, add lemon juice to stop the browning. Mix and remove. Pour over fillets.

Remove pin bones. Season fillet with salt and dust with flour. Shake off excess flour. Dip in whipped eggs and put into medium coarse bread crumbs mixed with equal parts of crushed almonds. Sauté over medium-high heat until golden brown on each side. Place in oven for 5 minutes at 375°.

Panfish Fritters

By Chef Charlie Gruss Serves 8 as an appetizer

1/2 lb panfish fillets (finely chopped)
1 cup. all purpose flour
1/2 tsp Kosher salt
1 tsp baking powder
peanut oil for frying

1/3 cup whole milk
1 egg
1 Tbsp melted butter

Sift together flour, salt and baking powder. Whisk in all other ingredients until smooth. Heat peanut oil to 275° and use household spoons to gently drop in approximately a spoonful of batter per fritter. Fry until dark golden brown and season with salt, immediately after removal from oil. Optional ingredients to add into this recipe: small diced white onion, minced parsley, chives, leeks, garlic, sweet corn, or minced jalapeño peppers. It's a versatile recipe, allowing for creativity and allows you to stretch out the results of a slow day of fishing.

Control Points

1. Oil temperature is very important. If the oil is above 275°, you risk burning the outsides of the fritters before the insides are fully cooked.

2. Stop mixing the batter as soon as you achieve smoothness. Overmixing will develop more gluten in the flour and make for chewy fritters.

3. Be very careful when dropping fritter batter into hot oil to prevent splashing hot oil on yourself.

FISH RECIPES

Oven Fried Crispy Walleye
By Pam Warnke

4 – 6-8 oz fillets
1 egg
1 3/4 cup crushed Club crackers
1/4 tsp salt
1/2 tsp paprika
1 tsp water
1/2 tsp onion powder
2 tsp fresh thyme
2 Tbsp lemon juice
1/3 cup grated Parmesan cheese
1 tsp melted butter

In a bowl, add cracker crumbs and melted butter and mix. Add all remaining dry ingredients and mix. In a separate bowl, mix egg, water and lemon juice. Dredge fillets in egg wash. Cover in cracker crumbs. Place in oiled baking dish and bake at 375° for 15-20 minutes.

Oysters Rockefeller
By Fremont Gruss Sr.

2 pints fresh oysters, drained
1 lb spinach, frozen chopped, thaw and thoroughly squeezed dry
10 slices of bacon, cook and crumble
1 small onion, diced fine
1 Tbsp garlic, diced fine
1 Tbsp butter
1 cup heavy whipping cream
1 Tbsp cornstarch
1/2 cup grated Parmesan cheese
2 oz Pernod liqueur

In medium saucepan, sauté onions and garlic in butter. Add cream, cornstarch and Pernod. Stir until mixture thickens. Add the squeeze dried spinach. Remove from heat. Add bacon and cheese. Cool.

Arrange oysters placed on the half shell on a baking sheet. Spread the cooled mixture on fresh oysters. Bake at 400° for 5 minutes or until cheese melts.

Perch & Crab Cakes
with Lemon Dill Pickle Tartar Sauce

By Chef Charlie Gruss

1 lb perch (chopped)
1/4 lb clarified butter
1/4 cup red onion (small dice)
1/4 cup coozed bacon (small dice)
2 Tbsp fresh parsley (minced)
Dash Old Bay dry seasoning
1 Tbsp Kosher salt
1 Tbsp fresh ground black pepper

1/2 lb canned crab meat
1/2 cup chives (minced)
1/4 cup mayonnaise
1 egg
1 cup Panko bread crumbs
1 Tbsp Dijon mustard
1 tsp garlic powder
2 Tbsp peanut oil for frying

Reserve 1/2 cup of the Panko bread crumbs, you will use these to roll your cakes in and reserve 2 Tbsp peanut oil.

Preheat oven to 350°.

Finely chop cleaned and de-skinned perch fillets. Gently combine all ingredients. Form 8 equal cake rounds and let rest for 15 minutes. (Mixture can be stored overnight)

Heat a sauté pan on medium heat, add peanut oil. Lightly brown on both sides. Lightly grease baking sheet. Put cakes on baking sheet, place baking sheet on the top rack of oven. Bake for 8 minutes and flip, bake an additional 8 minutes until done.

Control Points
1. Control your heat when sautéing to brown cakes; too high and cakes will burn.
2. Add dry seasonings (Old Bay, salt and garlic powder) by sprinkling from above to more evenly distribute into mixture.

FISH RECIPES

Skillet Salt Roasted Salmon with Lemon Confit

By Chef Charlie Gruss

Sauce

1/4 cup mayonnaise
1/4 cup dill pickle (small dice)
1 tsp Kosher salt
2 Tbsp dill pickle juice
1 Tbsp capers (chopped)
1 Tbsp lemon juice

Salmon

1-1/2 lb center-cut salmon fillets
(de-scaled, cut into equal portions by weight)

2 Tbsp extra virgin olive oil
1 Tbsp fresh dill (minced)
5 cups coarse sea salt
1 Tbsp fresh ground black pepper

Preheat oven to 400°. Heat 1 Tbsp of olive oil in an oven-proof skillet on medium-high heat. Add salmon skin side down and cook until the skin crisps (approx.. 2-3 minutes). Mound salt over each fillet and roast in the oven for 6 minutes for medium rare. Take out and brush the salt away. Transfer the salmon from the skillet and season with fresh ground black pepper, lemon confit, and drizzle with olive oil,. Garnish with fresh dill sprig.

Lemon Confit

6 lemons (sliced thin)
3 garlic cloves (minced)
1/8 cup sugar
3 shallots (minced)
1/2 cup Kosher salt

olive oil (to cover, amount dependent on size of container)

Boil water. Blanch lemons for 5 seconds. Cut off ends, slice very thin and remove seeds, set aside. Combine garlic and shallots. In a separate container combine salt and sugar. Layer bottom of a plastic storage container with lemon slices, sprinkle with garlic/shallot mixture, sprinkle with salt/sugar mixture. Repeat these steps until you finish with a salt/sugar mixture on top. Refrigerate mixture for at least 3 days. In a food processor, lightly pulse mixture together a couple of times. The mixture can be served or covered with olive oil and held in the refrigerator for 3 weeks.

Fish Fry Beer Batter
By Teri Gruss

1 cup flour
1 tsp sugar
1 tsp cayenne pepper
1 tsp garlic powder
2 lb fish fillets

1 cup cornstarch
1 tsp baking powder
1 tsp Old Bay seasoning
12 ounce bottle of beer

Combine dry ingredients in a shallow bowl. Add beer and mix until batter is smooth. Pat fish fillets or strips dry and dip in batter to coat. Fry in hot oil until golden.

Lake Trout
By Fatback McSwain

Clean and filet trout and cut into 1" chunks. Bring a mixture of 50% water and 50% 7Up to a full boil. Add fish chunks and boil for 10 minutes. Remove and place on a serving dish. Cover with a mixture of 1/2 cup melted butter and 1/4 tsp garlic powder. Pour premade salsa mixture over trout pieces. Bake at 375° for 45-60 minutes.

Salmon Fillets
By Tom Pearson at Camp Narrows Lodge

2 salmon fillets
3 cups sliced red onions
salt and pepper to taste

2 cups mayonnaise
garlic powder

Lay fillets in baking dish. Season with garlic, salt, pepper. Cover fillets with 1/2" of mayonnaise, place sliced red onions on top. Bake at 350° for 15 minutes.

Chapter 9

Smoking & Pickling Game and Fish

Smoked Jerky Venison
By Sarah Scholl

2 - 3-1/2 lbs of venison roast or steaks, sliced thin like bacon strips
6-7 oz soy sauce
2-3 oz water
1 tsp garlic powder
1 tsp Lawry's season salt
4 oz Worcestershire
3 tsp liquid smoke
2 Tbsp minced onion

Mix all ingredients and marinate 24 hours in refrigerator or overnight. Remove strips, pat dry and hang in top rack of oven. Bake at 375° for 4-5 hours.

Venison or Elk Jerky
By Richard Boser

3 lbs venison or elk. sliced 1/8" thick
1/3 cup Worcestershire
1/3 cup beer
1 tsp red pepper
1 tsp white pepper
1/2 cup brown sugar
1 tsp meat tenderizer
1/3 cup soy sauce
2 Tbsp salt
1 tsp black pepper
1/3 cup BBQ sauce
1 small bottle liquid smoke
1 tsp Kitchen Bouquet

Marinate meat in all ingredients for 12 hours. Place in dehydrator for 8 hours.

SMOKING & PICKLING RECIPES

Venison Jerky
By Donna Pittenger

2 lbs venison round steak, sliced in thin strips

Marinade
8 tsp soy sauce	5 tsp liquid smoke
1/2 tsp garlic powder	1/2 tsp onion powder
1/4 tsp black pepper	1/4 tsp salt

Marinade for minimum of 3 hours. Spread meat on racks and/or cookie sheets. Brush with remaining marinade. Bake 3-4 hours at 100° – 150°. Turn off oven, let stand overnight.

Smoked Pheasant Spread
By Sue Soderman

Smoke or obtain one large pheasant
8oz package of cream cheese	1/4 cup sour cream
1/4 cup finely diced onion	1/4 cup finely diced celery
1/2 tsp Lawry's season salt	dash of hot sauce

1 small garlic clove, minced finely
  and/or 1 small Jalapeño pepper, finely diced

Shred smoked pheasant pieces, add all ingredients from above and mix well. Allow to stand for 2 hours in refrigerator to blend flavors. Can be served hot or cold with crackers or French bread rounds.

Smoked Whitefish

By Kevin Fick
(works on toulibee too!)

Beer and molasses smoked fish brine
4 cups water
1 – 12-oz bottle of beer
1 tsp black pepper
1 tsp liquid smoke
3/4 cup salt
1/2 cup dark molasses
? tsp whole cloves
1/4 cup Worcestershire

4-6 whitefish, remove heads, slit stomachs and wash fish thoroughly (leave scales on). Mix all brine ingredients together. Place fish in plastic container and cover with brine over. Refrigerate for 24 hours. Place in smoker and heat on low for 4-6 hours.

Note: All smokers work differently. Use your favorite wood – hickory, apple, green button wood or whatever.

Smoked Cooked Wild Goose

By Tony Soderman & Bill Johnson, Wild Game Cookbook

6-8 lbs cleaned and plucked goose
2 cups salt
3 large apples, diced
1 cup diced celery
1/4 lb bacon slices
1 tsp ground sage
1 tsp salt
1 gallon water
1 medium onion, chopped
2 cups bread crumbs
2 Tbsp brown sugar
1/4 tsp thyme
1/4 tsp black pepper

Make a brine of the salt and water. Place goose in and leave for 10 hours in refrigerator. Remove goose, wipe dry and rub salt and pepper inside and out.

Fry bacon until crisp and crumble. Add to bread crumbs, thyme and sage, apples, celery and sugar into the bacon fat and sauté until apples are tender. Fill cavity with this mixture and sew shut. Cook goose at 325° on top rack with foil pan underneath. Cook 30 -35 minutes for each pound.

SMOKING & PICKLING RECIPES

Pickled Pike
By Brent Olson

2 lbs pike fillets
1 medium onion

1 qt white vinegar
1 lemon or orange

Day 1: Cut pike into bite size pieces. Soak pike pieces in a mixture of 3/4 cup pickling salt and 1 qt water in a non corrosive plastic container. (Make sure fish is covered with mixture) Soak for 24 hours.

Day 2: Remove fish and discard salt solution. Drain and rinse fish with water. Place fish back in container with vinegar and cover. Soak for 24 hours

Day 3: Drain and discard vinegar solution. Prepare brine.

Brine
2 cups vinegar
1 cup sugar

1 cup water
2 Tbsp pickling spice

Bring brine to a boil in sauce pan. Let cool to room temperature. Layer fish in 1 qt Mason jars, mixing in chunks of lemon or orange and onion. Cover with brine solution and cover. Flip or mix jars every two days. Fish is ready in 7 days.

Smoked Pheasant Breast
By Morgan Smith

Marinate pheasant breast (bone in or out) in Jack Daniels teriyaki sauce for 2-3 days. Smoke for 1 hour at 180° (baste with remaining sauce). Smoke until meat thermometer reads 165°. Remove from smoker and eat hot or let cool.

Venison Roast Marinade
By Randy "Layout" Fetterman

2 cans beer
lemon pepper
bacon bits
liquid smoke (to taste)

1/2 cup vinegar
garlic powder
salt and pepper

Adjust to size of roast to adequately cover.

Make small cuts in roast, rub in lemon pepper, garlic powder, salt, pepper and bacon bits.

Marinade roast in solution for 24 hours in refrigerator.

Low-fire water smoker for 5-6 hours

Smoked Mallard
By Rob Anderson (Douglas County Duck Guide)

2 quarts water
4 oz pickling spice
1 lb. brown sugar
1 cup dark molasses

2 cups apple vinegar
1/4 cup non-iodized salt
1 Tbsp liquid smoke

Mix all ingredients together in a plastic container. Put in plucked mallard and refrigerate over night. (12-24 hours). Slow cook on Holland type grill or smoke on top shelf of smoker for 3-1/2 - 4 hours.

SMOKING & PICKLING RECIPES

Venison Jerky (Brined & Cured)
By Chef Charlie Gruss

1 venison top round or flank steak

Trim off excess fat, partially freeze meat, and cut into thin slices, 1" to 1-1/2" in thickness, with the grain.

Brine
1 gallon water	1 lb Kosher salt
3-1/4 oz white sugar	1 oz pickling spice
4 garlic cloves (minced)	

Place meat slices into brine and refrigerate for 45 minutes. Halfway through the brining process, stir the meat slices around to ensure even brining. After 45 minutes, rinse the meat well and pat dry.

Cure
2 tsp onion powder	2 tsp garlic powder
2 Tbsp ground white pepper	2 tsp paprika
2 Tbsp ground black pepper	

Place cure in a shaker and apply evenly over both sides of the meat. Place slices on a lightly oiled smoking rack. Let dry for 1 hour and smoke between 75° – 90° until the jerky snaps when bent. Usually between 10-12 hours. For a meatier jerky, cut smoking time in half.

Control Points
1. The slices must be kept thin to allow the brine to effectively penetrate the meat in 45 minutes.

2. Cut the meat with the grain. This will allow you to cut the grain with your teeth when chewing.

Venison Kielbasa Christina

By Chef Charlie Gruss Yield: 5-1/2 lbs sausage

3 lbs venison scraps (cut into 1/2" cubes)
2-1/2 lbs pork butt (cut into 1/2" cubes)
1 tsp Instacure (nitrates)
2 Tbsp salt   2 tsp sugar
2 tsp ground black pepper   1 tsp fresh marjoram (chopped)
2 tsp coriander seed (cracked)   12 cloves garlic (minced)

Combine all ingredients and mix well. Refrigerate mixture for 1 hour. In a meat grinder, run mixture through large hole plate. Take half that amount and run through the small hole plate of the grinder. Mix the two different grinds together and mix in a stand mixer with a paddle attachment for 30 seconds on low speed. Stuff into size 30-32 hog casings and form 8-inch sausage lengths.

Control Points
When grinding sausage it is important to keep grinding equipment as cool as possible. It's helpful to freeze meat grinder attachments prior to use.

Chapter 10
Sauces, Side Dishes & Other Unique Recipes

Pheasant Stock

By Pam Warnke

4-6 pheasant legs
1 onion
1-2 carrots
1-2 ribs celery (cut into 1" slices)
peppercorns
1-2 potatoes
garlic
bay leaf
salt

Place all ingredients in a stock pot, cover with water and bring to a boil. When stock boils, turn down to low and maintain a slow gentle simmer. Simmer until meat readily comes off bones. Strain stock, remove meat from bones. (For a more concentrated stock, simmer longer) Can be frozen for 3 months. Use in your favorite soups. Tip: Pour in ice cube try and freeze. Place cubes in freezer bag. When needed, use 2-3 cubes for stock flavor.

Duck Glaze

By Glenn Gausman (long time member of the Earl Oxley Camp)

1 small can frozen orange juice
1 banana, mashed
1/2 cup Karo white syrup

Mix together and cook over low heat. Use the mix to glaze ducks or goose being baked on a charcoal grill.

Multiple Game Marinade

By Buckshot, Chuck Johnson

1/2 cup soy sauce
3 Tbsp brown sugar
1 onion, chopped
3/4 cup white vinegar
1 tsp ginger

Soak for half hour.

Spice Mix for Duck
By Chef Charlie Gruss   Makes 1 cup

1 oz Kosher salt
2 oz anise seed
1 oz nutmeg
2 oz black peppercorns
2 oz clove

Combine all ingredients except salt and grind in a clean coffee bean grinder. Store in an airtight container for 6 months.

Spice Blend for Wild Game
By Chef Charlie Gruss   Yield 17.03 ounces

1 lb Kosher salt
.175 oz fresh ground black pepper
.088 oz dried marjoram
.138 oz ground nutmeg
.175 oz dried thyme
.138 oz bay leaf
.175 oz juniper berries
.138 oz powdered ginger

Combine all ingredients, except Kosher salt and grind in a clean coffee bean grinder. Mix into salt. Store in an airtight container for up to 6 months.

Wild Game Meat Marinade
By Don Schroeder

1-1/2 cups salad oil
1/2 cup wine vinegar
1/4 cup Worcestershire
2-1/2 tsp salt
2 tsp fresh chopped parsley
3/4 cup soy sauce
1/3 cup lemon juice
2 Tbsp dry mustard
1 Tbsp coarsely ground pepper
2 cloves garlic, crushed

Combine all ingredients and mix well. I like to marinate meat overnight. Makes about 3-1/2 cups. Store marinade in tightly covered jar in refrigerator or freeze if not used immediately. Makes the best ribs!!

Orange Sauce For Ducks or Geese
By Dave (Mambo) Manley

1 cup sugar
2 Tbsp cornstarch
1/4 cup lemon juice
1 Tbsp butter
1/4 tsp salt
1 cup orange juice
3/4 cup boiling water
1 tsp grated orange peel

Combine all ingredients, except butter and orange peel. Bring to a boil for 1 minute. Add butter and orange peel.

Pesto Sauce
By Teri Gruss   Makes 1 cup

2 cups fresh basil leaves
3 Tbsp pine nuts
1/2 tsp sea salt
2 cloves garlic, peeled
1/2 cup olive oil
1/2 cup grated Parmesan cheese

Place all ingredients except cheese in a food processor. Puree until smooth.

Transfer to a bowl and stir in grated cheese. Should have the consistency of a smooth paste. Great over pasta, on toasted French bread or straight out of the bowl.

Mexican Dip
By Kim Dewey

1 package Jimmy Dean sausage, browned
1 can Rotella tomatoes
8 oz cream cheese
bag of corn chips

Combine browned sausage, tomatoes and cream cheese. Place in crock pot on low-medium. Serve with corn chips.

Chicken Wings
By Paulette Dalum

3/4 cup maple syrup
1/4 tsp dry mustard
ginger (to taste)

1/4 cup soy sauce
garlic powder (to taste)

Mix ingredients. Place chicken wings in baking dish and pour mixture on top.

Bake at 450° for 1 hour.

Venison Cream Cheese Appetizer
By Banquet Attendee 06

8-oz cream cheese
1/2 lb venison sausage, browned

1 can Rotella tomatoes
bag of corn chips

Mix cream cheese, tomatoes and browned sausage together. Put in small crock pot and heat on low. Serve with chips.

Spiral Sausage Appetizer
By Brian Ingals

1 pkg puff pastry, thawed
1 pkg spicy pork sausage

Lay out puff pastry. Spread cooked and cooled sausage over evenly. Carefully roll dough mixture in a spiral and place in freezer for 30 minutes. Take out, cut into 3/8" slices and place on baking sheet. Bake at 425° for 10 minutes.

Sweet & Tangy Barbeque Sauce
By Dave "Dancin" Manley

Makes 3 cups

2 cups ketchup
4 Tbsp mustard
4 Tbsp Worcestershire
2 Tbsp Tabasco
2 cloves minced garlic
1/2 tsp cayenne pepper

2 medium onions, quartered
1 cup molasses
4 Tbsp cider vinegar
1/3 cup olive oil
2 Tbsp chili powder
3 tsp liquid smoke

Puree onion and 1/2 cup water in food processor for 45 seconds. Strain in wire mesh strainer to capture 1 cup of onion juice. Add ketchup, molasses, mustard, Tabasco, Worcestershire, vinegar, black pepper and liquid smoke in a saucepan and apply medium heat until simmering. Add garlic, cayenne pepper, chili powder stir well and mix for 45-60 seconds. Continue heating until mixture thickens and allow to cool before using.

SAUCES & SIDE DISHES

Dry Rub Barbeque
By Banquet Attendee 07

1 Tbsp black pepper
1 Tbsp sugar
2 Tbsp cumin
1 Tbsp oregano
3 Tbsp garlic powder
2 Tbsp sea salt

2 tsp cayenne pepper
2 Tbsp brown sugar
2 Tbsp chili powder
4 Tbsp paprika
1 Tbsp white pepper

Mix all ingredients together. Store in plastic container in refrigerator or freezer until ready to use.

Venison Polish Sausage Barbeque
By Jim Knudsen

2 cups ketchup
1 cup bourbon

1 cup brown sugar
6-8 Venison polish sausages

Cut polish sausage up into 1" chunks. Mix all ingredients in a sauce pan and bring to a boil. Cover and simmer for 2-3 hours, stir every few minutes. Place in serving dish and use toothpicks.

Shrimp Salad
By Donna Pittenger

2 cups small shell macaroni
1 cup sour cream
1/4 cup sugar
2 cans salad shrimp

1/2 cup mayonnaise
1 small onion, chopped
salt and pepper to taste
green pepper, chopped

Cook macaroni, rinse and cool. Mix all ingredients. Add to macaroni and chill before serving.

Orange Almond Salad
By Barb House

1/2 head lettuce
1/4 cup slivered almonds
2 Tbsp sugar

Dressing
2 Tbsp vinegar
2 Tbsp sugar
1/4 tsp almond extract

1 cup diced celery
1 Tbsp onion
1 sm can mandarin oranges, drained

4 Tbsp salad oil
1/2 tsp salt
dash pepper

In small saucepan, combine almonds and sugar. Stir until almonds are coated and delicately brown. Cool and break apart. Add all other ingredients. Pour dressing over salad just before serving.

Easy Fruit Salad
By Banquet Attendee 06

2 cans tropical fruit
3 Tbsp dry Tang
1/2 pint fresh cut up strawberries

1 med can chunk pineapple
1 box instant vanilla pudding
1 banana

Drain pineapple and save juice. Combine juice, pudding mix and Tang to make dressing mixture. Drain tropical fruit. Stir tropical fruit into dressing mixture along with the rest of the fruit. Chill and serve.

Cold Spaghetti Salad
By Jennifer Bjorklund

1 box spaghetti
1/2 green pepper, diced
1/2 yellow pepper, diced
1 can sliced black olives
4 green onions, sliced including greens

1 pint cherry tomatoes, halved
1/2 red pepper, diced
1 sm pkg pepperoni, cut into 1/4s
1 bottle Italian salad dressing

Cook spaghetti as directed and rinse. Put spaghetti in bowl. Add vegetables, pepperoni and Italian salad dressing. Refrigerate overnight.

SAUCES & SIDE DISHES

Caribbean Cole Slaw

By Barb Gerling

1 medium head red cabbage, quarter and thinly slice/chop
1 large red pepper, diced
1 bunch green onions, chopped
4 carrots, diced
1 cup green olives with pimento, sliced
1 Tbsp celery seeds

Toss vegetables and seeds together to make slaw.

Sweet and Sour Vinaigrette
1 cup olive oil
1/4 cup sugar
1/4 cup red wine vinegar
salt and pepper

Mix well and pour over slaw. Chill before serving.

Harvest Red Cabbage and Apples

By Teri Gruss

1 medium head of red cabbage, thinly sliced
3 slices bacon
1/2 medium onion, chopped
2 medium apples (Fuji are good)
3 Tbsp sugar (or honey)
3 Tbsp cider or plum vinegar
   (Add more if you like a tart sweet and sour sauce)
salt and pepper, to taste

Bake bacon in oven till crisp, about 10 minutes. Put bacon drippings in a large skillet or stockpot. Add cabbage, onions and apples. Stir fry until they are barely tender. Add sugar and vinegar. Heat on low until sugar dissolves. Stir in crumbled bacon.

Spinach Salad with Homemade Dressing
By Teri Gruss

1 lb fresh spinach
1 cup red onion
4 oz Swiss cheese
8 slices bacon
3 hard boiled eggs

Thoroughly wash spinach. Tear into bite sized pieces. Bake bacon at 400° until crisp, about 10 minutes. Chill and crumble. Peel, chill and crumble hard boiled eggs. Thinly slice red onion. Grate cheese. Combine all, toss and chill.

Dressing
1 cup virgin olive oil
1/3 cup catsup
2 tsp Worcestershire
3/4 cup sugar
1/4 cup apple cider vinegar

Whisk together in a large bowl until well mixed and smooth. Chill.

Grilled Red Onions
By Tom at Camp Narrows Lodge

1 large red onion per person
butter
olive oil
blue cheese chunks

Peel outside skin from onion, core out a hole in top that is approximately 1" at top and 1/4" at bottom. (make sure not to cut all the way through the onion, leave 3/4" uncut on bottom). Make a mixture of 1/4 butter and 3/4 of blue cheese chunks. Stuff mixture into onion hole. Wipe olive oil on outside of onions and wrap in tin-foil. Place on top rack of grill and slowly bake for 45-60 minutes

SAUCES & SIDE DISHES

Bunch Corn
By Jim "Big" Bunch

2 eggs
1 stick melted butter
1 can creamed corn

8 oz sour cream
1 Jiffy corn muffin mix
1 can regular corn

Mix all ingredients. Turn into greased 3 quart baking dish. Bake at 350° for 45-60 minutes.

Mayonnaise Biscuits
By Banquet Attendee 07

1 cup self rising flour
2 Tbsp mayonnaise

2/3 cup milk
4 Tbsp cooking oil

Carefully add milk to flour and mix. Add mayonnaise and mix thoroughly. Put 1 tsp oil into each muffin cup pan. Fill cups half full with mixture. Bake at 350° for 15 minutes.

Popovers with Honey Butter
By Banquette Attendee 07

Popovers
3 eggs
1 cup milk
2 Tbsp melted butter
1 cup all purpose flour
1/2 teaspoon salt

Honey Butter
1/2 cup softened butter
2 Tbsp honey

Preheat oven to 425°. In a small bowl, beat eggs at medium speed until foamy. Blend in milk and butter. Add flour and salt. Beat at low speed until blended (about 3 minutes).

Fill greased popover pan/muffin cups, or 6 oz custard cups half full.

Bake at 425° for 35-40 minutes. For crispier popovers, prick side of each with wooden toothpick and bake additional 3-6 minutes.

Overnight Buns
By Gwen & Jim Risbrudt (3M camp chefs)

1 pkg yeast
1 cup sugar
2 eggs, beaten
3 cups warm water
1/2 cup melted shortening
9 cups flour

Start at 5pm. Mix yeast, warm water, salt, sugar, eggs, flour and shortening. Knead and punch down every hour until 10pm. Shape into rolls, set in cool place and cover. Bake in morning at 350° for 13-15 minutes.

Whipping Cream Rolls
By Donna Pittenger

2 Tbsp margarine
1 pkg frozen dinner rolls
3/4 cup brown sugar
1/2 pint whipping cream

Mix margarine and brown sugar until crumbly. Place in bottom of a 9x13" baking pan. Arrange frozen dinner rolls on top of sugar mixture. Pour whipping cream over rolls and refrigerate overnight. Bake at 350° for 30 minutes. Let stand 30 minutes before turning out of pan

Beer Bread
By Banquet attendee 05

3 cups self rising flour
12 oz beer (warmed to room temperature)
1/4 cup sugar

Mix the flour and sugar. Gradually add the warmed beer until dough is pliable and well blended. Pour into greased loaf pan and bake at 375° for 1 hour. Guys love it! It's very hearty, crusty and a heavy bread that goes well with stews.

SAUCES & SIDE DISHES

Molasses Bread
By Gwen & Jim Risbrudt (3M camp chefs)

3 cups scalded milk
3/4 cup brown sugar
1-1/2 tsp sugar
1-1/2 Tbsp salt
1-1/2 cups graham flour
2 pkgs yeast

3 cups cold water
1/2 cup melted shortening
1/2 cup molasses
1-1/2 cups rye flour
white flour
1/2 cup warm water

Mix ingredients. Let rise 1 hour. Knead well. Put in baking tins, let rise. Bake at 350° for 40 minutes.

Best Ever Belgian Waffles (Easy overnight method)
By Teri Gruss   Makes 8 waffles

2-1/2 cups warm milk
1 tsp sugar
1 tsp salt
2 cups unbleached all purpose flour
1/4 tsp baking soda

1 pkg regular yeast
8 Tbsp (1 stick) butter, melted
2 eggs, beaten

In a large bowl mix 1/2 cup milk, yeast and sugar. Let stand for 5 minutes. Add melted butter, remaining milk, salt and flour. Stir to blend. Place in a large plastic pitcher with a lid. Let stand at room temperature overnight. It should double in volume.

When ready to make waffles, stir in beaten eggs and baking soda. The batter should be smooth and somewhat thin. Preheat waffle iron. Use between 1/2 to 3/4 cup batter for each waffle. This depends on the size of your waffle iron.

Batter will keep in refrigerator for about 3 days. This is a great recipe to make ahead of time when you are having company.

Swedish Pancakes
By Sue & Gramma Soderman

3 eggs
1/2 cup sugar
1/2 cup milk
melted butter

1/2 tsp salt
1/2 cup cream
1 cup flour

This batter is very thin. Mix all ingredients except flour. Slowly add the flour and beat in. Melt butter in an 8" skillet. Add approximately 1/4 cup of batter and immediately lift and twist pan to cover bottom of pan with thin batter. Flip pancake when bottom is brown. Swedes spread the pancake with butter and sugar, roll up and eat. Whipped cream and fruit stuffed inside is also very good "der too don't cha no!"

Egg Bake
By Dan Davids

7 oz box of croutons
1 lb ground venison
1 can cream of mushroom soup
2-1/4 cups milk

2 cups shredded cheese
6 eggs
3/4 tsp dry mustard

Grease 9x13" baking pan. Brown the ground venison in skillet. Place venison in bottom of pan, then the cheese, then the croutons.

Mix eggs, dry mustard, milk and pour over crouton/venison mixture. Place in refrigerator overnight. Take pan out in AM and combine 1 can mushroom soup with 1/2 cup milk. Pour over egg mixture and cook at 300° for 1-1/2 hours.

Breakfast Soufflé

By Barb House

12 eggs, beaten
4 cups milk
12 slices bread, cubed (stuffing bread also works)
2 tsp salt
2 tsp dry mustard
1 tsp onion powder
2 cups cheddar cheese, shredded
2 cups ham (bacon, turkey or pheasant), already cooked
1/2 cup green pepper

Whip eggs, milk and seasonings. Mix meat, bread and cheese and put in a greased 9x13" baking pan. Pour egg mixture over bread mixture. Best if set overnight in refrigerator

Bake at 350° for 45 minutes. Eat with or without salsa (heated).

A great addition is adding Montreal seasoning, either chicken or steak, depending on the meat you use.

Corn & Onion Pudding

By Pam Warnke

1-1/2 cups fresh yellow corn
1/2 cup chopped red pepper
3 eggs, beaten
1/2 cup Parmesan cheese, grated
pinch garlic powder

1 large yellow onion
1/2 cup chopped green pepper
1 cup half & half
salt and pepper
pinch onion powder

In a large skillet add 2-3 Tbsp olive oil (or half oil, half butter). Add onions and sauté until golden brown. Put onions in a shallow baking dish, then add peppers, half & half, seasonings, and beaten eggs. Sprinkle cheese on top and bake for 35-40 minutes at 400°. Last 3-5 minutes, turn broiler on to brown top. Let cool and serve.

Sweet Potato Hash
By Chef Charlie Gruss

4 lg sweet potatoes (diced small)
1 red onion (diced small)
1 red pepper (diced small)
2 garlic cloves (rough chopped)
10 strands chives (minced)
2 Tbsp oil
1 fennel bulb (diced small)
3 celery stalks (diced small)
1 cup maple syrup (warmed)
2 sprigs parsley (minced)
6 strands tarragon (minced)
salt and black pepper to taste

Preheat oven to 400°. Cut sweet potato and place on oiled baking sheet. Bake for approximately 12 minutes, until golden brown. Cut all other ingredients, except fresh herbs. Bring a large sauté pan with 1 Tbsp oil to smoking hot, turn heat down to medium-high. Add in this order: onion, fennel and garlic. Sauté for 1 minute then add celery, red pepper and cooked sweet potatoes. Mix well. Add minced fresh herbs. Add maple syrup. Lightly season with salt and pepper. Taste and adjust seasoning. You could also add a few tablespoons of unsalted butter to finish for more flavor.

Control Points
Knife cuts of your ingredients are important from a presentation standpoint. Diced Small means 1/4" x 1/4" x 1/4". Mince means to cut into fine indiscernible sized pieces. Rough Chop with garlic in this recipe would mean about the size of a small dice.

Crock Pot Stuffing
By Donna Pittenger

12 oz herb stuffing (Kellogg's Croquettes)
1 cup butter or margarine
2 cups celery, chopped
2 cups onions, chopped
4 cups broth or bouillon
parsley
mushrooms
2 eggs, beaten

Sauté the butter, parsley, onions and celery. Place all other ingredients in crock pot and add broth. Cook on high for 1 hour and turn down to low for 4 hours.

Wild Rice Casserole
By Anne Gruss

1 cup wild rice
1/2 cup olive oil
1-1/2 cup boiling water
1 cup canned, diced tomatoes
2 cloves garlic, crushed
1 cup cheddar cheese, grated
1 cup sliced mushrooms
1 cup sliced onions
1 cup sliced black olives
salt and pepper to taste

Rinse wild rice and put in a casserole dish. Pour boiling water and olive oil over rice. Add all remaining ingredients to wild rice and mix well. Cover with lid or foil and bake at 350° for one hour. Remove cover. Stir. If liquid has not completely absorbed, return to oven for several more minutes.

Green Apple Cake
By Gwen & Jim Risbrudt (3M camp chefs)

2 cups sugar
2 eggs
2 tsp soda
1 tsp cinnamon
1 tsp cloves
1/2 cup walnuts, cut fine
1 tsp vanilla
1 cup butter
1 cup cold coffee
2 cups sour green apples
1 tsp nutmeg
3/4 cup raisins
3-1/2 cups flour

Mix all ingredients, place in baking pan.
Bake at 350° for about 40 minutes or until done.

Frosting
1 cup brown sugar
1/4 cup cream
powdered sugar
1/2 cup butter
1 tsp vanilla

Melt together butter and brown sugar. Add cream and boil 2 minutes. Cool and add vanilla. Add enough powdered sugar to reach desired thickness.

Oatmeal Cake with Broiled Coconut Frosting

By Teri Gruss

Cake
1-1/3 cup boiling water
1 cup oatmeal
1/2 cup butter
1 cup white sugar
1 cup brown sugar
2 eggs
1-1/3 cup flour
1 tsp baking soda
1 tsp salt
1/2 tsp cinnamon
1 tsp vanilla

Frosting
1-1/2 cups brown sugar
6 Tbsp butter
1 t vanilla
1/4 cup cream
1/2 cup chopped pecans
1/2 c shredded coconut

Pour boiling water over oatmeal. Let stand for 15 minutes. Beat butter with white and brown sugar. Add eggs, oatmeal, flour, baking soda, salt, cinnamon and vanilla and mix together. Pour into a 9x13" baking dish and bake at 325° for 30-35 minutes.

Combine all frosting ingredients and spread on warm cake. Broil for about 5 minutes, or just until frosting melts and coconut stirs golden brown.

Bernes Brulee (Fresh Berry Brulee)

By Karen Weunberg

Fill a 9x13" baking dish to the top with a mixture of fresh berries (strawberries, raspberries, blueberries, lingonberries, cranberries).

In a bowl, mix 1 cup sour cream with about 6 oz of cream cheese. Add 1 Tbsp brown sugar. Thoroughly mix until no lumps remain.

Spread like a frosting over berries. Liberally sprinkle additional brown sugar over the frosting. Broil on low setting until the brown sugar starts to melt and bubble.

Bread Pudding with Amaretto Sauce

By Teri Schenke – Bogy Bayou, Florida

Pudding
1 cup golden raisins
1 cup Amaretto
8 Tbsp butter (one stick)
1/2 tsp each cinnamon and nutmeg
4 eggs
1 Tbsp almond extract
12-oz can evaporated milk
1-1/2 cups water
12 slices of day old bread

Sauce
8 Tbsp butter
1-1/2 cups powdered sugar
1/4 cup Amaretto

Soak raisins overnight in Amaretto. Drain. Preheat oven to 325°. Melt butter with sugar in skillet over medium heat. In a bowl mix eggs, spices, almond extract, evaporated milk, water, raisins and butter/sugar mixture. Stir to thoroughly blend ingredients.

Break the bread slices into a buttered 9x13" baking dish. Pour liquid mixture over the bread. Bake for 1 hour.

Melt the butter and powdered sugar together in a saucepan over medium-low heat. Remove from heat and add 1/4 cup Amaretto.

Serve pudding and sauce warm.

Peanut Butter Crunch Cake
By Barb House

1 yellow cake mix
1 cup creamy peanut butter
1/4 cup vegetable oil
6 oz pkg. chocolate chips
1/2 cup packed brown sugar
1 cup water
3 eggs
1/3 chopped nuts (optional)

Heat oven to 350°. Grease and flour 9x13" baking pan. Beat dry cake mix, brown sugar, and peanut butter on low speed, scraping bowl constantly until moistened. Reserve 2/3 cup. Add water, oil and eggs, beat on medium speed for 2 minutes. Pour batter into pan. Stir nuts into reserved crumbly mixture and sprinkle over batter. Sprinkle with chocolate chips. Bake until cake springs back when touched lightly in center, 40-45 minutes.

CHAPTER 11
Nutritional Aspects of Wild Fowl and Game
By Teri Lee Gruss, MS Nutrition

I had no idea what wild duck, goose, pheasant, grouse, venison, elk, moose, antelope or caribou tasted like, much less the nutritional value of these meats until I started dating my husband-to-be Brad Gruss back in 1969.

I grew up in a family of non-hunters and the only meat and fowl that we ate we got at the grocery store! Brad and his enthusiastic family of sportsmen, hunters and fishermen all, and his mother Karen Gruss, a creative and accomplished cook have all been instrumental in teaching me the value and pleasure of cooking and eating wild fowl and game.

It was a brave new world that I entered the first time I visited the Gruss hunting camp called Fremont's Point on Big Mantrap Lake in Park Rapids, Minnesota. I had never seen my food hanging from nails on the side of a cabin or split open and hanging from a tree!

While studying nutrition in school I learned just how much healthier a regular diet of wild fowl and game can be compared to eating commercially raised poultry and beef.

There are several very important advantages of a wild waterfowl and game diet including reduced exposure to growth hormones and antibiotics regularly used in commercial poultry and meat production. Growth hormones are primarily used to increase the weight of animals. These hormones also increase the amount of saturated fat in animal tissue. Over time, the consumption of these substances may disrupt our own hormonal balance, although this subject is controversial. Long term consumption of antibiotics in meats and poultry may increase our resistance to pharmaceutical antibiotics used to treat bacterial infections.

LAKE CHRISTINA COOKBOOK

In general, wild waterfowl and game are lower in calories and saturated fats than commercially raised poultry and meats. While we require some saturated fat for health, most, but not all, wild meats appear to have a healthier fat ratio of saturated, monounsaturated and polyunsaturated fats compared to "grocery store" meats.

Nutritional Comparison of Wild Fowl

SPECIES	CALORIES	PROTEIN	CARBS	TOTAL FAT
Wild Duck	211	17 g	0	15 g
Domestic Duck	404	11 g	0	39 g
Domestic Chicken	172	21 g	0	9.2 g
Pheasant	181	23 g	0	9 g
Wild Goose	138	11.4 g	0	10 g
Domestic Goose	371	16 g	0	34 g
Venison Tenderloin	149	30 g	0	2 g
Elk Tenderloin	111	23 g	0	1.5 g
Beef Tenderloin	358	23 g	0	29 g

3.5 ounce serving (g=grams, mg=milligrams)

CHAPTER 11

This comparison illustrates that wild fowl and game, in general contain less calories and saturated fats than their commercial counterparts. Where the animal forages and how it is cooked, in the end, affects its overall nutrient profile.

and Game versus Domestic Meat

SATURATED Fat	MONO-UNSATURATED Fat	POLY-UNSATURATED Fat	OMEGA-3 FATTY ACID	OMEGA-6 FATTY ACID
5 g	6.8 g	2 g	170 mg	1850 mg
13 g	18.7 g	5.1 g	390 mg	4691 mg
2.7 g	3.8 g	2 g	120 mg	1740 mg
2.7 g	4.3 g	1.2 g	100 mg	810 mg
3.1 g	4.6 g	1.1 g	NA	NA
9.8 g	17.8 g	3.8 g	210 mg	3340 mg
1 g	6 g	1 g	27 mg	76 mg
5 g	4 g	3 g	40 mg	170 mg
12 g	12.2 g	1.1 g	280 mg	750 mg

Source: USDA Standard Reference 20
Analysis is on meat and skin, raw
Small naturally occurring amounts of trans fats not included

Often wild game is considered to be a good source of omega-3 essential fatty acids but in fact, wild fowl has very high concentrations of omega-6 fatty acids. Animal flesh, in general, contains a much higher concentration of omega-6 fatty acids, which, in excess, promote inflammation and may increase risks for cardiovascular disease. Fatty fish is nature's richest source of omega-3 fatty acids.

In my opinion, today our best, safest source of essential omega-3 fatty acids is distilled fish oil, guaranteed free of mercury and other toxins like PCBs. These fats are "essential" because our bodies cannot manufacture them.

A large body of scientific research indicates that including adequate amounts of omega-3 fatty acids in our diets promotes the normal growth and development of children and reduces our risks for a long list of inflammatory, degenerative conditions including cardiovascular disease, arthritis, neurological disorders including depression, anxiety and more.

Another less discussed and more controversial difference between wild and commercially raised fowl and meats is that of our exposure to genetically modified organisms in our food supply. Ultimately what the animal eats, we eat!

Genetically modified (GM) organisms are plant or animal cells that have been altered using genetic technology, most often to achieve herbicide tolerance and insect resistance. This modification creates cells and tissue that have never before existed in nature and therein lies the controversy.

The technology is usually called recombinant DNA technology. This simply means that DNA (the genetic blueprint of a cell) is taken from different sources and combined to make a new molecule of DNA. In 1996, scientists introduced genetically

CHAPTER 11

modified organisms into our food supply when they created plants capable of tolerating certain herbicides.

According to the U.S. government's Human Genome Project, "In 2006, a total of 252 million acres of transgenic (genetically modified) crops were planted in 22 countries by 10.3 million farmers. The majority of these crops were herbicide and insect-resistant soybeans, corn, cotton, canola and alfalfa. 89% of planted soybeans and 61% of corn grown was of genetically modified origins." Other GM crops being tested include wheat, rice and sweet potato.

The Grocery Manufacturers of America note that "approximately 75% of all processed foods in the U.S. contain a GM ingredient." Corn, in the form of high fructose corn syrup, and soybean oil account for a large portion of our food supply exposure to genetically modified organisms and the chemicals used on them in the field.

A large portion of soy and corn crops are used in animal feed. Currently our government does not require labeling of any GM sourced foods.

As well as not requiring a label on genetically modified foods, our laws largely prohibit the labeling of non-genetically modified foods. A growing number of lawsuits have been filed by companies that use non-GM foods in their products and want to label them accordingly so the public can make an educated choice in what they eat. In 2001, Japan required that foods of GM origin must be labeled.

Early in 2008 the Monterey California County Agricultural Committee considered a ban on GM crops in Santa Cruz. Will we see GM crop bans in the U.S.? Will Congress step forward to initiate labeling of these products? Do genetic scientists truly understand the long term health implications of eating a diet high in genetically modified organisms? Do we understand the environmental threats to insects like bees, wildlife and aquatic life living on and near GM crop fields?

My intent in presenting this information on genetically modified organisms is to hopefully heighten an awareness of our growing exposure to genetically modified foods. To date, there is no scientific agreement as to the long-term safety of consuming organisms that have never before in the history of the universe existed, or been eaten in such mass by humans.

As we all strive to be healthy; to avoid obesity, heart disease, diabetes and cancer, among other degenerative diseases, the nutritional differences between wild and commercial fowl and meat are more important than ever.

Wild fowl and game provide a rich source of protein, help us cut excess calories and saturated fats from our diets, and reduce our exposure to hormones, antibiotics and genetically modified organisms found in commercially raised animal meats. Those are exciting benefits from a nutritional point of view!

I count myself and my family very fortunate to have such a diverse source of wild waterfowl, game and fish in our freezer at season's end each year.

Wishing you and your families many happy trails and long and healthy lives.

Chapter 12
Making a Difference
By Brad Gruss

I recall very vividly that fall day in 1998 when Harvey Nelson and Howard Norby came to the back door of this old hunting cabin. I knew of both Harvey and Howard as they had hunted the lake for many, many years together as boys growing up in this area. As Harvey began to inform me of their intent to establish a lake association to help fix the lake and improve habitat, my first thought was "Why?" What good would it do? How could we make a difference?

I had no idea of Harvey's presence and long established work history in the U.S. Fish and Wildlife Service (USFWS). He had served all over the North American continent in his pursuit of helping ducks and wildlife. He went on to explain that unless government knew there was a unified voice of a couple hundred people, a voting block if you will, the bureaucrats would simply ignore a few hunters complaining about low duck numbers. This was the key moment in our decision to get behind this start-up group. It made sense! Maybe we could do something?

Harvey went on to explain that there were thousands of dollars and hundreds of government programs available if there was a voice to be heard. He mentioned Ducks Unlimited. I've been going to DU functions for over 30 years, but rarely did I see first-hand what they can do until it happened right here at Lake Christina. He mentioned Minnesota Waterfowl Association, Delta Waterfowl, Coots Unlimited, Pelican Lake Association, Evansville Sportsmen's Club, Stalker Lake Sportsmen Club, and a whole host of organizations which might help, if we just got organized.

The point here is that if you live near a good hunting area and have seen a decline in opportunities, or if you have been traveling great distances each fall to pursue game and hunt duck, geese, deer, turkey, pheasants or big game, all with declining habitat and huntable numbers, you should get involved! It is not easy. It takes time. You have to work with many government institutions that move so slow it makes you want to give up! A lot of the hurdles are created by bureaucracy and the elusive chase of our government dollars.

If you are a businessman or somewhat of an action-type person, you typically define a problem, collect data, lay out the possible course of action, and make a decision to act! It doesn't work that way when you are involved with government. Don't get me wrong here, it CAN BE DONE. It takes effort, time, thick skin and a whole lot of dedicated people to make it happen.

"Make a Difference." Get involved. Start a lake association. Join DU or another group which is active in your kind of outdoor activities. For that matter, if you are a hunter and not a member of the NRA, shame on you! Start a local sportsman group. Search out those who care about habitat, wildlife, the shooting sports and the great family tradition it offers.

We did it on Christina! We are not done yet, but have seen great improvements in water quality and duck numbers. We have a plan to fix the problems that have slowly eroded hunting opportunities in the last 30-50 years. Early on, our Minnesota Department of Natural Resources (MNDNR) was seen as the obstacle — "the do nothing state organization." It was a poor relationship with many locals complaining of their inactivity.

We jointly established a working group of our CIA Board, Ducks Unlimited, MNDNR biologists, USFWS representatives,

CHAPTER 12

county land managers, NDSU Research Biologists and began to meet on a regular basis. What did this do? It showed to many that we wanted to be part of the resolution, we wanted to get things done, we wanted to show that we could work within the realm of how government works. Some members complained early on that nothing was getting done, that the work group meetings were a waste of time, that the DNR would not move forward. Guess what? It does work! You must first establish trust, you must show that it takes science and data collecting and a lot of behind the scene work. We have formed a great relationship with our MNDNR. We know they listen and together we are all on board with the goal of solving the root cause issues that have destroyed many lakes, potholes and sloughs in this important region.

Ducks Unlimited has been the driving force in time, effort, money and overall guidance to our CIA Board and membership. They have spent well over a million dollars on engineering, establishment of fish structures, and professional guidance. We have been very fortunate to have so many DU engineers, biologists and managers on our side and guiding our direction. I and many of our members have increased our donations and status as life members because of their continuous efforts. DU is not just a banquet and fund raising party! They get things done when they see you have a groundswell of support. Many people within our CIA group have worked hard for over 10 years now to get to where we are. Why? Because you can make a difference and reach goals that not only improve habitat and hunting numbers, but offer our kids and our grandkids a chance to share in the beauty of the outdoors. Get involved. Go make a difference. It can become a reality.

Wildlife Utilization of Lake Christina

Sometime after the late 1800s, early 1900, canvasbacks began to concentrate on Lake Christina in increasing numbers. From shortly after the turn of the century to the early 1950s, it was renowned as a fall concentration area. It was especially well known as a feeding and resting area for divers, particularly canvasback. Available information indicates that Lake Christina's best years were those of the late 1930s and 1940s. The following is a brief synopsis of fall waterfowl use trends on Lake Christina.

The number of waterfowl, principally canvasback, would range from 40,000 to 60,000 birds. Peak coot numbers would range from 200,000 to 300,000 birds during this same period. Total numbers of all species of waterfowl utilizing the lake were estimated at 300,000 to 400,000 birds. Following the peak of 60,000 canvasbacks in 1942, the canvasback population using the lake decreased until 1949 when the largest concentration of canvasback ever witnessed on Lake Christina occurred.

This largest concentration of canvasbacks was documented in the 1950 *Quarterly Game Research Report* in Volume 9, Number 4. A total count of 800,000 waterfowl was obtained. Of this number, 80% or approximately 640,000 were coots. It was estimated that 160,000 ducks were present, of which 100,000 to 150,000 were canvasbacks.

Since the 1950s, canvasback usage of Lake Christina has declined due to poor water and vegetation quality along with rough fish populations and high water conditions. Management of the lake, along with periodic fish kills every 10 years or so, has brought the lake back to a more favorable condition. In 1994 the canvasbacks one again returned with numbers peaking at 105,000 of a total bird population of 695,000 on October 20.

CHAPTER 12

Following this chapter are the Minnesota Department of Natural Resources tabulation sheets for aerial duck counts during 1994 and 2007. When you compare the 1994 numbers of canvasback to the 2007 numbers and the total duck counts, it is apparent that the installation of water level control devices is critical to saving the "King of Ducks." With proper funding, and at the urging of waterfowlers everywhere, we hope to accomplish this goal in 2010.

The last hurdle and main goal of this lake group is to install water level control pumps and an outlet mechanism. This will allow periodic drawdowns to eliminate or minimize rough fish populations and promote the vegetation and food necessary for migrating ducks. This, we hope, will eliminate the use of chemicals like Rotenone every 10 years or so. Controlling water level and promoting a sound food resource will insure that Christina continues to be that special place for canvasbacks well into the future! The current outlook is that it will be done in 2010. It will be a huge expense to engineer, purchase, install and maintain. This technology is proven and after being successful here, we hope that it can be done on several critical duck staging lakes up and down the flyway. It may be the single most important cure for the future of waterfowling and we encourage you to not only support our goal, but consider this course of action for your own important duck habitat and resting areas.

Thank you for purchasing this cookbook! It will help canvasbacks and other diver ducks for sure, as well as helping the CIA efforts move forward in conservation and restoring water quality and habitat.

Wishing you safe hunting and plentiful future opportunities to enjoy the outdoors and shooting sports.

LAKE CHRISTINA COOKBOOK

LAKE CHRISTINA 2007
MINNESOTA DEPARTMENT OF NATURAL RESOURCES
DIVISION OF GAME & FISH
GF-83 Rev. 6/73

TABULATION SHEET

	9/24	9/27	10/1	10/11	10/22	10/29	10/30	11/07	11/08
CANVASBACK	320	650	750	2,000	4,000	1,400	1,200	65	400
REDHEAD	900	1,000	2,000	1,250	2,000	2,000	2,000	200	240
SCAUP			400	600	7,000	500	600	225	220
RING-NECK	400	800	5,000	7,000	10,000	15,000	15,000	350	2100
GOLDENEYE						20			
BUFFLEHEAD					100	40	1		5
RUDDY DUCK	30				200	30			
UNIDENTIFIED							25,000*	2,200	15
MALLARD	650	300	220	400	1,300	240	3,600	800	165
BLACK									
PINTAIL	4								
GADWALL	120				220		650		
AM. WIDGEON	175	25	20	180		40	400		
BW TEAL	450		200						
GW TEAL	225		200		4				
WOOD DUCK	375			70				2	
SHOVELER				50		5		9	
TOTAL DUCKS	3,649	2,775	8,790	11,550	24,824	19,275	48,451	3,851	3,130
CANADA GOOSE	80	100	350		200	370	150		75
SNOW GOOSE									
SWAN		2	5	6		3		39	
HOODED MERG.									
R.B. MERG.									
C. MERG									20
COOT	100,000	260,000	200,000	150,000	150,000	100,000	100,000	1,800	330
TOTAL BIRDS	103,729	262,877	209,145	161,556	175,024	119,648	148,601	5,690	3,555
WESTERN GREBE	125		20		20		45		
BALD EAGLE	3							8	
CORMORANT									
OTHER: PBG	55								
% ICE COVER	0	0	0	0	0	0	0	35	90
PLANE	BOAT	C185	C185	C185	C185	C185	BOAT	GROUND	C185
PILOT	—	PFINGSTEN	PFINGSTEN	PFINGSTEN	PFINGSTEN	PFINGSTEN	—	—	PFINGSTEN
OBSERVER	CARLSON	HANSEL-W	HANSEL-W	HANSEL-W	HANSEL-W	HANSEL-W	CARLSON	CARLSON	HANSEL-W
PASSENGER	CALL	—	—	—	—	—	WEBB		
TIME	0900	1300	1230			1120	0945	1030	1300
SKY	●	○	○		○	○	○	●	●
WIND	SW ●15	NW ●20	CALM		NW 10-15	CALM	CALM	S 15-20	CALM

* 10/30: BIRDS CAME IN EVE OF 10/29, 25,000 UNIDENTIFIED DIVERS LEFT IN A "TORNADO" WHEN WE PUT ON THE LAKE.

CHAPTER 12

LAKE CHRISTINA — FALL, 1994

MINNESOTA DEPARTMENT OF NATURAL RESOURCES
DIVISION OF GAME & FISH

GF-83
Rev. 6/73

TABULATION SHEET

	SEPT 15	SEPT 22	SEPT 29	OCT 5	OCT 13	OCT 20	OCT 26	NOV 3	NOV 10
CANVASBACK	600	550	1,000	1,700	70,000	105,000	32,000	4,200	2,100
REDHEAD	200	200	600	1,500	18,000	37,000	2,500	200	55
SCAUP			350	400	2,000	3,000	5,500	1,400	1070
RING-NECK	1,100	3,200	10,500	29,000	30,000	52,000	10,500	7,500	2450
GOLDENEYE									12
BUFFLEHEAD					200		200	15	10
RUDDY DUCK		35	20	150	300	200		250	
MALLARD	560	700	600	200	3,000	5,500	1,500	210	60
BLACK									
PINTAIL	15			30	50				
GADWALL	150	400	500	1,000	2,000	2,500		40	40
AM. WIDGEON	1,650	1,250	1,800	4,500	5,000	4,000	500		240
BW TEAL	1,400	50							
GW TEAL									
WOOD DUCK	50	20		10					
SHOVELER				10					
TOTAL DUCKS	5,725	6,405	15,270	38,500	130,550	209,200	52,700	13,815	6,037
CANADA GOOSE	55	80	20	130	85	1,740	315	125	2
SNOW GOOSE						10			
SWAN									5
HOODED MERG.					40				10
R.B. MERG.									
C. MERG.									
COOT	9,000	27,000	42,000	140,000	220,000	390,000	52,000	7,500	11,100
TOTAL BIRDS	14,780	33,485	57,290	178,630	350,675	600,950	105,015	21,440	17,154
WESTERN GREBE	115	39	81	7	69	50	5	1	
BALD EAGLE	3	3	0	1	2	0	2	2	
CORMORANT	125	35	30						
OTHER:	1 OSPREY	10 PELICAN							
% ICE COVER	0	0	0	0	0	0	0	0	0
PLANE	C185	C185	C185	C185	C185	C185	C185	C185	C185
PILOT	STOLTMAN	STOLTMAN	STOLTMAN	STOLTMAN	STOLTMAN	STOLTMAN	STOLTMAN	STOLTMAN	STOLTMAN
OBSERVER	LARSON	BRYSON	CARLSON	CARLSON	CARLSON	LAWRENCE	LAWRENCE	CARLSON	CARLSON
PASSENGER	-	-	-	-	-	-	-	-	-
TIME	0945	0935	0930	1350	0930	1300	1345	1015	1030
SKY	●	◐	○	●	○	◐	○	●	●
WIND	S @ 15	NW @ 20	SE @ 5	SE @ 15	SE @ 10	CALM	SE 20	S @ 10	S @ 25

LAKE CHRISTINA COOKBOOK

Left to right: Tom Carlson, MNDNR; Brad Gruss, Banquet Co-Chairman; Bud Grant, Retired Minnesota Viking Hall of Fame coach

Tom Carlson, MNDNR biologist and 30 year Christina veteran received the prestigious CIA BULL CAN AWARD from Bud Grant in 2006 at the September Fundraiser Banquet, for his great efforts, strong support and great partnership with the CIA.

Prestigious Bull Can Award

An award given annually to the person who has shown great effort, enthusiasm and action in promoting the goals of the CIA, improving habitat or motivating others to get involved.

2000	Duke Anderson
2001	John House
2002	Jon Schneider
2003	Kevin Fick
2004	John Lindquist
2005	Brad Gruss
2006	Tom Carlson
2007	Mike Evavold
2008	Greg Lillemon

Bull Canvasback shot on Millionaire's Point circa 1945

If you love canvasbacks, you should support this lake association. It doesn't matter if you hunt them in Chesapeake Bay or the whole East Coast, Lake Erie, Michigan, Ohio, New York, or in Texas, Florida, Louisiana or Canada.

Christina, when healthy, holds up to 20% of the North American continent's canvasback population during the spring and fall migration. This lake is a strategic holding, resting and feeding lake. It helps them to find the food necessary to make their long journey. Approximately two-thirds of Christina is a NO MOTOR ZONE during the hunting season providing a huge expanse of water where they can feed, rest and remain unmolested. The Christina, Ina, Anka Lake Association is working hard to restore this lake and refuge and we need your help. Buying this book is helping canvasbacks.

Ducks Unlimited, has been the leader in wetlands restoration for the whole North American continent. All duck lovers and sportsmen should recognize their terrific value. Please consider supporting DU and Lake Christina in a generous way. Large contributions sent to DU can be specified directly to and for Lake Christina. Smaller contributions can be sent directly to the CIA. Should you have any questions, contact your state DU staff person or Jon Schneider, Manager Minnesota Conservation Programs at jschneider@ducks.org

"Thank You"

MISSION STATEMENT

Christina Ina Anka Lake Association
Box 402
Ashby, Minnesota 56309
Non-Profit 503C Corporation, ID # 41196771

MISSION STATEMENT

Improve and maintain water quality and preferred aquatic food resources so as to restore lakes Christina and Anka as important fall staging areas for waterfowl.

Determine appropriate fish management programs for each of the three lakes.

Consider alternatives for reduction of rough fish populations.
- The need for better water level management to permit periodic draw-down to enhance control of rough fish and growth of aquatic plants and invertebrate populations in lakes Christina and Anka
- The need for better understanding of the hydrologic budgets for these lakes
- The need for updating lake management plans to address current problems in further detail

A non-profit 503C corporation, dedicated to improving water quality, duck habitat, and the future of the outdoors.

Make a difference, get involved and make a donation.

To order additional copies of this book, send requests to:

CIA COOKBOOK
Christina Ina Anka Lake Association
Box 402
Ashby, MN 56309

or email bradgruss@hotmail.com

Cover illustrations by John House

Front: "Cans flying by the Christina Mountain"

2009-2010 CIA Board Members

John Lindquist

Brad Gruss

Jim Knudsen

Greg Lillemon

Tom Warnke

Andy Lang

Tom Soderman

"Once upon a time, Christina was a migratory stop for 800,000 waterfowl including 100,000+ canvasbacks. An invasion of rough fish and high water turned Christina into a shallow bowl of nothing. The restoration launched in the last decade has reclaimed Christina so that more than 260,000 waterfowl returned in the fall."

"Supporting this lake association and fixing this strategic canvasback resting and migratory sanctuary is critical to the "King of Ducks" ... and maybe, diver duck hunting!"

"A wonderful collection of historic accounts relating to the chase of the mighty canvasback, a cookbook of game and fowl recipes that shows the emotion and care that hunters have for both restoring a hunting treasure and enjoying it on the table."

Harvey Nelson, USFWS (retired)